D0324209

WITHDRAWN
FROM THE COLLECTION
CARNEGIE LIBRARY OF PITTSBURGH
CLP-

Carnegie
Library of
Pittsburgh
Main

SUZUKI EDUCATION IN ACTION

Suzuki Education in Action;

A Story of Talent Training From Japan

Clifford A. Cook

MT1.C72
Cook, Clifford A., author.
Suzuki education in action;
a story of talent training
from Japan
New York, Exposition Press
[c1970]

MUSIC ROOM

An Exposition-University Book

Exposition Press   *New York*

AUG 3 1978

Carnegie Library
of Pittsburgh

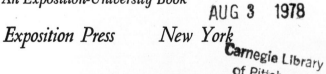

I 80

Second Printing, August 1975

© 1970 by Clifford A. Cook

All rights reserved, including the right of reproduction in whole or in part, in any form or by any means, electronic or mechanical, including photocopying, recording, or by any information storage and retrieval system, without permission in writing from the Publisher. Inquiries should be addressed to Exposition Press, Inc., 900 South Oyster Bay Road, Hicksville, N.Y. 11801.

Library of Congress Catalog Card Number: 74-136977

ISBN 0-682-47192-5

Printed in the United States of America

Dedicated

to

SS *by* CC

Contents

Preface

After more than ten years of acquaintance and rich experience with Suzuki Talent Education, plus newly acquired freedom from the tyranny of the teacher's wrist watch, it is both a pleasure and a duty for me to write this book. The pleasure comes from reflection on a huge accumulation of memories—mostly happy ones—of the people, ideas, and personal experiences connected with this subject. The sense of duty or obligation comes from awareness of my great debt to many friends—from Shinichi Suzuki down to my most recent little beginner on violin—who have given of themselves so generously that I must do my best to pass on both their gifts and my own observations.

Much has been written in English during the past decade about the subject of this book. Some of it is authentic, much is either second- or third-hand or based on little knowledge of the subject, and some of it is fallacious. I hope that my present contribution to the literature, based on extensive personal contact with Mr. Suzuki and his teachers and students, plus my own teaching experience, may prove a valuable addition. To be frank, though, I must admit that Rudyard Kipling had a point in his famous statement about the East and West. I believe that no American will ever fully understand Suzuki Talent Education.

The chapters are in roughly chronological order, beginning with the first article I had published on Talent Education. The last chapter details my connections with Talent

Education from 1958 into 1970, and my final conclusion as to the value of the movement.

Apologies are due to many Americans doing outstanding work in this field who are neglected in my book. Such neglect is not due to lack of appreciation; I have simply tried to write about what I know rather than what I don't know.

Readers will note the repetition occurring in the book. Repetition is a most important principle in the Suzuki way of teaching; "once over lightly" has no place in the system. Mr. Suzuki has often said that he hopes to live to the age of one hundred so he can repeat his message over and over until it is finally understood.

Intelligent repetition, aimed at improving the understanding and performance of music, is basic all the way from the beginner studying his first piece to George Szell studying the score of a Beethoven symphony for the thousandth time. *It works.*

Acknowledgments

Certain chapters are reprints of articles of mine which have appeared in various publications. Several chapters include excerpts from others of my previously published articles. Scattered throughout the book there are also a few selections from publications of other writers, or statements made to me personally. Such items are noted as they occur, and gratitude is hereby expressed to all these generous sources for their kindness and help.

My thanks go to Kenji Mochizuki for first acquainting me with the Talent Education movement in Japan. Mr. and Mrs. Shinichi Suzuki and the Japanese teachers and students have given me far more than I can ever repay. My wife has been most helpful in her suggestions and in typing the manuscript.

For my good American friends—children and their parents, fellow teachers, all those who supported and encouraged my work through the years—my appreciation is deeper than I can express. To all these, Japanese and Americans, my grateful thanks and my hope that this book may give you some small pleasure, as you have given me so much!

—CLIFFORD A. COOK

Oberlin, Ohio
1970

Chapter I

*Japanese String Festival—1955**

For many year I have heard that the Japanese are not
gifted in playing our Western string instruments and that
they are imitators in many fields. I was, therefore, a bit
skeptical when, in the spring of 1958, Mr. Kenji Mochizuki
asked if I would be interested in a sound film and tape of
a Japanese string festival. Kenji was at that time a student
in the Oberlin Graduate School of Theology; he was also a
violinist who played in my College-Community string festival. We arranged a time for an "audition."

The film and tape were impressive. Huge numbers of
Japanese children were playing from memory violin music
ranging up to the level of the Vivaldi and Bach double concertos. Aside from the sheer weight of numbers and the
appeal of cute tots performing seriously, the outstanding
features for the string specialist were these: (1) There was
not a poor left-hand position or bow arm visible in the
entire group. (2) Intonation was good and pleasing tone
was modulated expressively. In short, this was not just mass
playing of 1200 children from five to thirteen years of age—
it was *good violin playing!*

I arranged for Mr. Mochizuki to show his film and speak
to my classes and to appear before the Ohio String Teachers
Association meeting in Oberlin in May of 1958. These
appearances aroused considerable interest in the Japanese

*Reprinted by permission from the *Music Educators Journal* of November—December, 1959.

string movement; the film has since been shown at Inter-
lochen, Los Angeles, New York, Toronto, and other places.
One Ohio string teacher, John Kendall of Muskingum College, saw the film in Oberlin and became so interested that
he went to Japan in the summer of 1959 to investigate the
teaching that produced such remarkable results.

The string festivals held each spring for the last few
years represent one phase of a postwar movement in Japan
known as "Talent Education." There are other phases, such
as art and ballet, but we are concerned here with the study
of violin by young children. Mr. Mochizuki, Dr. Masaaki
Honda, Director of Talent Education, and President Shinichi
Suzuki (the violin teacher who is the originator and guiding
genius of the string movement) have been most generous
in conversation, correspondence, and provision of many programs, pamphlets, pictures, as well as the complete set of
volumes of the *Suzuki Violin School.* One of my students,
Miyako Matsuki, has been helpful in translating some pas-
sages from the original Japanese.

Mr. Suzuki, after the Second National Assembly in 1956,
wrote:

> If I had said ten years ago that I was going to have a group of
> over one thousand children, ages between five and thirteen, play
> Vivaldi's *Concerto* or Bach's *Double Concerto,* I don't think there
> would have been a single person in this world that would have
> believed me.
>
> Right after the war, when there were still many remains
> of destroyed buildings all over the city, I started this talent
> education. I started it because I realized how much these inno-
> cent children were suffering from the dreadful mistake made
> by the adults. These precious children had absolutely no part
> in the war and yet they were the ones suffering the most severely,
> not only in food, clothing and a home to live in, but also some-
> thing that was very important, their education.
>
> I was teaching violin before the war and I found to my
> amazement that children show talent far beyond what their

parents or the world expect of them. As long as they have normal mental ability to learn, it has been proven that any child can be taught to play the violin.

However, there are two important factors. Young children have the natural ability to conform to atmosphere very easily. Therefore if we lose this period of life it is most difficult to teach the violin and get the same kind of result. Another important thing we must remember is that children learn by repetition. When we repeat one thing many times, this becomes a part of the child as his own talent. Watch the child learn his first word. His mother repeats the same word over and over to make him hear and learn it. But very soon these words will become a part of the child and this same child in a few years will be speaking the language so fluently that it may sometimes surprise his own parents or friends.

I applied this theory in teaching violin and taught to all children Bach, Vivaldi, Handel and Mozart. Soon children learned to play many pieces by hearing the tune repeated many times and finally memorized the entire work.

Through this work the thousand children that gathered from all over the country were able to play together without having had any rehearsal. It is really not such a surprising thing.

We are not teaching these children to make them professional musicians. I believe sensitivity and love toward music or art are very important things to all people whether they are politicians, scientists, businessmen or laborers. They are the things that make our lives rich.

I am praying that the day will come when people all over the world will have truth, righteousness and beauty in their lives.

It is evident that Mr. Suzuki is a humanitarian as well as a highly-skilled violin teacher and psychologist. Let us examine a few points in his statement. He believes in the universality of musical talent and in the importance of giving expression to it at an early age. Over and over in his writings we find reference to the way the very young child learns to speak his native language, use of the same method to learn musical language, and suggestions about the employment of the violin as an instrument for expression of musical language. Use of recordings, along with the fact that assisting teachers throughout Japan have all been trained by Suzuki, provide uniformity in the performance of the children when they come together for the Festival.

Is this entirely a rote method? This is one of the questions asked most frequently. No. Strict rote learning is used only in the early stages, according to Mr. Mochizuki. Reading from notation is introduced in due time; the *Suzuki Violin School* includes eleven volumes at present, plus some supplementary ones. The music, editing, and pedagogical plan are all of high quality, solid and sound. Mr. Suzuki is a violinist who knows his business. Although he is not attempting to discover and educate artists, he has, nevertheless, produced some. Toshiya Eto, concert artist and teacher at the Curtis Institute in Philadelphia, is one example. There are others of distinction.

Instruction is given once a week at a cost of about $2.73 per month. Daily home practice is supervised by an interested family member who also attends the lessons. In fact, the criticism has been made that parents sometimes become too interested. (Many American string teachers who have had their students told by parents to "go to the cellar or attic to practice that thing so we won't hear it" wish they had more reason to make the same criticism!)

Mr. Suzuki claims that practically any child of six, after a year of lessons, can play a Seitz "Concerto" almost perfectly. The performance of the children in his string festivals shows that his claims must be taken seriously. Perhaps Mr. Suzuki and a representative number of Japanese youngsters might appear at one of our MENC national meetings?

Mr. Ragnar Smedslund, Consul General of Finland in Japan, after hearing the 1955 National Concert, wrote:

The scene is Tokyo's new Sportshall on a Sunday in March. The galleries are full of 10,000 spectators who, spellbound, are following the spectacle in the arena where 1200 violin playing

Chapter II

National Concert in Japan*

The Ninth Annual General Concert of the Talent Education Institute was held in the Yokohama Culture Gymnasium on March 30, 1963. Usually in Tokyo, the festival site was changed due to extensive construction in preparation for the 1964 Olympics. Before an audience of about six thousand nearly two thousand children from many sections of Japan performed at various times in a tripartite program lasting from 1:00 to 5:15 P.M.

Graduation Ceremony

After a short speech by President Shinichi Suzuki of The Talent Education Institute, he presents diplomas which he had designed to the 508 children aged from five to fifteen years, who graduate this year. (There are three graduation levels; Mr. Suzuki hears a tape from each candidate, then writes his criticisms and reasons for graduating the child or not.)

Approximately one hundred teachers stand before the children during the ceremony. Greetings are given by Mr. Yoshichika Tokugawa, Honorary President of Talent Education, and by Mr. Kaneshige Tanaka, Chief of the Committee. Then all the graduating students play the first movement of the Vivaldi *Violin Concerto in G minor*. Many children had played a more difficult concerto for their graduation re-

*Reprinted by permission from *The School Musician* of August-September, 1965.

children of the age of 4 to 15 are playing Vivaldi's Concerto in A-minor. In the middle of the arena there is a platform with a grand piano and on the four sides thereof the youngest children are lined up.

The program was commenced by the first movement of Mozart's Violin Concerto in A-major played by the 80 most advanced violinists. Thereupon, 120 of the next lower class joined them for playing the first movement of Bach's Concerto in A-minor. And for each new item on the program a new group marched in until the total reached 1200. After the Vivaldi "Concerto" the program consisted of various selections of Bach, Lully and Handel.

Behind this concert there is an all-Japan organization for "the education of the children's talents." It has its headquarters in Matsumoto, Nagano Prefecture, and 65 branches in various parts of Japan. The total number of pupils is at present about 4,000. The founder and leader of this organization is a well-known violin teacher, Shinichi Suzuki, who naturally conducted this concert.

Everyone who was present at the concert in Tokyo Sportshall must have found it an eloquent testimony of the possibilities of bringing to light and developing children's talents at a tender age. And everyone of the audience is no doubt willing to subscribe to the statement by William James quoted in the program as follows:

"Compared with what we ought to be we are only half awake. We are making use of only a small part of our physical and mental resources. Stating the thing broadly the human individual thus lives far within his limits. He possesses powers of various sorts which he habitually fails to use."

Is it possible that Professor James' statement may apply to teachers and students in our country? I believe so. The Japanese String Festival delivers the message!

quirement, but they all unite in playing this one. Mr. Suzuki
starts them, then they're on their own without a conductor.
They do a beautiful job and richly deserve their flowers and
bows at the conclusion.

The Children's International Goodwill Gathering

Following messages by the Governors of Kanagawa Prefecture and of Yokohama City, there is a fanfare by a United
States Navy Band, seated on the stage and conducted by
Mr. Herbert Weber. Then seventy-two children play the
first movement of Mozart *Violin Concerto No. 4 in D* with
piano accompaniment by Mrs. S. Suzuki. I recognize a nine-
year-old boy in the group, but there are probably many
younger children. This performance is excellent.

Next, about four hundred children play a Weber "Country Dance" with fine staccato bowing and brilliant sound.
The band accompanies this piece. Then about six hundred
children, including some four-year-olds, play the first movement of the Vivaldi *Concerto in A minor.* The piano is on
stage; the children are spread out on the floor of the gymnasium. The ensemble becomes ragged (there had been no
rehearsal and there is no conductor), so Mr. Suzuki has
the huge group repeat this number while he conducts. Stay-
ing together is a problem with such large numbers of children
spread over a big area.

Two rows of young cellists then play Suzuki's "Variations on Twinkle, Twinkle, Little Star." The smallest children, age four or five, sit on little chairs and use tiny cellos.

Now about 1,200 child-violinists, with conductor and
band, play Schumann's "The Two Grenadiers." On stage with
the band are seated an American Elementary School Choir
and a Japanese High School Girls' Choir, both from Yokohama. After they have sung several selections separately

under their conductors, Miss Roush and Mr. Murayama, they combine with the violins and band in Handel's "Chorus" from *Judas Maccabaeus*. The sound is thrilling.

Mr. Suzuki speaks briefly on his favorite subject, "The Happiness of All Children," followed by the "Goodwill Exchange by Foreign and Japanese Children." Flags of all countries are carried to the center of the hall by Boy and Girl Scouts. Mr. Suzuki then conducts all in the hall in singing and playing his "Children's Happiness," which uses the "Twinkle" tune in triple meter, with a nice little obbligato violin part for advanced players. During this performance, tiny children carrying flowers—in pairs, a Japanese and a foreign child holding hands—march through the avenue of flags.

Then more tiny fiddlers crowd across the front of the stage, until the entire hall is packed with children and violins. What a sight and sound as they all play "Papillon" (better known to us as "Lightly Row")! Then one of the violin teachers, Mr. Hirose, leads everyone in the hall in singing and playing "Annie Laurie." This concludes the second part of the program.

Does some of all this sound "corny?" It isn't, it's *touching*. What is really "corny" is sophisticated insincerity!

The Annual Grand Concert of Talent Education Students

Mrs. Cook and I are honor guests at the Yokohama concert; my short speech is translated into Japanese by Dr. Masaaki Honda. An excerpt from this talk follows:

Since September we have traveled many thousands of miles throughout Europe and America, and we have heard all the playing of string instruments we could possibly hear. We believe that in no other country we visited are as many young children playing violins so well as here in Japan. In the life of the spirit and in the field of education, what you are doing for children in Talent Education stands out as impressively and beautifully as does your lovely Mt. Fuji!

All three movements of the Bach *Concerto in A minor* are then played by 250 or more children, some of them very small. A teachers' string orchestra, conducted by Mr. Nishizaki, plays along with the children. The tone and shading, the musical quality of this performance are almost unbelievable to a Westerner.

Mr. Suzuki then leads about 640 children in the first movement of the Bach "Double Concerto." Many of the children (some five years old) appear tiny on the floor of the large gymnasium, but they perform with the style of finished artists.

After the Band has played "Foster Rhapsodie," arranged by Newell Long, more children pour on to the floor until more than 1,200 are there. With band accompaniment they play a Mozart "Polonaise," the familiar "Waltz" of Brahms, and a Bach "Menuetto" in two parts (No. 2 in Volume I).

For the closing pieces, still more children with violins (including three-year-olds) jam the entire floor and fill all available space on the stage. There must be well over 1,500 by this time. With solid tone and delightful bowing style they play "Warnung" and the "Variations on Twinkle Twinkle." This mass of young fiddlers is the cutest thing I have ever seen or heard!

The closing number is "Auld Lang Syne," played and sung by all the people in the hall. Thus ends an afternoon I'll never forget; the concert still seems like a fantastic dream. Six weeks of visiting Talent Education branches throughout Japan are later to show us the same fine quality of performance in solos and smaller groups, but as an introduction to first-hand observation of the movement it would be hard to top the exciting impact of the Ninth Annual General Concert in Yokohama!

Chapter III

A Summary of My Impressions of Talent Education in Japan[*]

There is nothing really new or unorthodox in the ideas underlying the Talent Education (Saino-Kyoiku) movement, and yet the whole movement is new and unorthodox. This paradox is one of many confronting the visitor from the West. The strange mixture of East and West in Japan produces fascinating results, not always easy to comprehend.

Starting planned education at a very early age, providing a stimulating musical environment, emphasizing the ear, encouraging maximum participation by the child—examples of the use of this method are numerous and they span centuries. Consider Wolfgang Mozart, Jascha Heifetz, and all the others we call prodigies. Did not their parents follow such procedures?

From time immemorial every infant who has learned to speak his *mother tongue* (well named!) has done so by the method now labeled Talent Education. As Mr. Shinichi Suzuki points out, the child's speaking achievement is not gained by using formal, written etudes, but through the natural and obvious method of imitating his mother and other members of his family.

By applying to violin playing the principles used in teaching young children to speak their language, Mr. Suzuki has proved that much of what we have assumed to be in-

[*]Written after our six-week visit to Mr. Suzuki and his centers in Japan in 1963. Pamphlet printed in Tokyo, and distributed there at the Conference of the International Society for Music Education, July 4, 1963.

born genius in the prodigy-violinists has actually been a rather common talent which has been stimulated and developed by a favorable environment from a tender age.

In seventeen years of application of the principles of Talent Education, Mr. Suzuki and his teachers have proved with thousands of young children that *talent is common, favorable environment is not.* The responsibility lies with parents and teachers.

Listening to the young Japanese children play, one soon forgets their ages and the fact that they are playing music performed elsewhere by high-school and college students. There is alert vitality and complete involvement in what they do. (Mr. Suzuki says he wants not music education, but *musical* education.)

An overwhelming impression comes from the beautiful tone many of the children produce, from the intensely musical quality of their performance, and from the sweet and pure expression they have. Anyone not touched by such children and their playing has a hard shell, indeed!

Although the aim is not to produce professional musicians, many fine young artists have come up through this system and more will come in the future. The empirical approach is used; everything must be tested, compared, and proven.

Recordings by fine artists take care of many details, leaving the teacher free to concentrate on a few bonus items. Much of the "private" instruction given is actually before a group, using the European class method,* and playing together is a regular feature for the students. The concours or contest type of competitive motivation is not used in Talent Education.

One student at a time is given a lesson, observed by a group of auditors.

Teachers come together regularly to discuss and improve their work; close communication is maintained among all the people connected with the movement in various ways.

The extra-musical aims of Talent Education are idealistic, almost religious. Emphasis is placed on "heart," on making a better world through better people, on international goodwill, on "The Happiness of All Children." Talent Education people show much interest in helping the handicapped, such as a blind boy-violinist, a moron-artist, artists who must paint with mouth or foot.

Doctors, professors, engineers, many excellent people in varied fields take an active part in the movement, and getting to know these people and their families provides genuine pleasure for the visitor. They are practical idealists of the finest kind.

A few experiments in teaching mathematics, foreign languages, and other subjects along the Talent Education lines have been introduced. The full implications and applications of the principles are still to be realized, however, and the only limitations lie in the imagination and ingenuity of teachers who apply the principles to fields other than violin playing.

There are criticisms of Talent Education, of course. Many are due to ignorance, misunderstanding, vested interests, or vested ideas. Some criticism is justified to a degree—there are weaknesses, especially in carrying out the principles. For example, at times during unrehearsed ensemble playing by many children with no conductor, a lack of "togetherness" may tend to spoil somewhat the over-all effect of very good individual performances by the children. But the many strengths of this educational movement greatly outweigh any weaknesses in carrying out details.

Mr. Suzuki, always the idealist, has generously and unselfishly provided fertile fields for many other people to cultivate; such is his nature. He says "It is not enough to try to prevent the use of the nuclear bomb; *we must do something helpful for people everywhere!*" In my opinion, what he has done for young children earns him a place among the benefactors of mankind, along with such men as Albert Schweitzer, Pablo Casals, and Tom Dooley.

As a string teacher with many years of experience and thought, now completing a sabbatical year of travel and observation in Europe, the United States, and Japan, I offer my sincere opinion that Mr. Suzuki's Talent Education program appears to me to be the most significant and promising development in string education today. Furthermore, I believe firmly that his method and ideas deserve investigation and study by teachers of *all* subjects!

Chapter IV

Saino-Kyoiku

The following account of Saino-Kyoiku—Talent Education —was given as part of a program for The Oberlin Woman's Club on September 27, 1963. Shortly thereafter about thirty young children were started on violin study by this method.

About seventy-five years ago in Nagoya, Japan, the first violins made in that country were produced by a gentleman named Masakichi Suzuki ("Suzuki" is roughly the Japanese equivalent of "Smith" in America). His founding of a violin factory indicated the awakening interest in Western music. The history of Western music in Japan is thus comparatively short and recent.

Mr. Suzuki accounted for a dozen children as well as many violins. One of his sons, Umeo, is now President of the violin factory in Nagoya. (A violin from that factory was shown—10th size, suited to a three or four-year-old child.) Another son makes violins by hand in Matsumoto. Many of the Suzuki children were musical; in fact, a string quartet composed of four of the brothers toured extensively in Japan and developed a considerable reputation there.

Our story today concerns one of the twelve Suzuki children, Shinichi, now sixty-five years old. He began the study of violin in Japan with Miss Ando and later studied for eight years in Germany with Professor Klingler. He heard Fritz Kreisler play in Berlin, and has continued to hear the "Kreisler tone" on records ever since. It has been his model and ideal.

After returning to Japan Shinichi Suzuki taught violin in

Tokyo, Yokohama, and other centers, according to conventional methods. The first very young child he taught was Toshiya Eto who began study at the age of four. But this was before the Talent Education ideas had fully developed in Mr. Suzuki's mind.

When, during World War II, the bombing of Tokyo became severe, Mr. Suzuki went up into the mountains where he lived with a sister and her infants. As the food rations became smaller and smaller, he gave his share to the children and began foraging for anything he could find to eat. Leaves from trees and other such "foods" caused malnutrition; he later became very ill, and was almost given up as lost by his doctor. Just in time, however, it was discovered that he could digest a kind of rice. This pulled him through a long convalescence.

During his convalescence Mr. Suzuki had had time to reflect on the horrors of war and how innocent children were its pitiable victims. He also had observed how his sister's babies learned to talk. As he pondered these things he determined to do something for the children he pitied so much. Since the violin was his life, he decided to devote himself henceforth to teaching little children how to play it well and thus give them the satisfaction and happiness which music had given him. He hit on the idea of teaching children to play violin according to the same method by which they learn to talk. Thus, about seventeen years ago, the movement now called "Talent Education" was born after a "pregnancy period" of some thirteen years.

Mr. and Mrs. Suzuki settled in Matsumoto, near the Japan Alps, and the beginning of Talent Education there consisted of five or six children and one violin. He began working on his method; it took about five years to get things going, and he spent ten years finding the right combination of material for Book I of the method. This was no period of miracles; it was rather a time of groping to find the correct foundations on which to build. A slow, careful beginning period has remained basic in this method.

Gradually, as Suzuki lectured throughout Japan and finally had some children who could demonstrate the success of his ideas, he began to attract attention. Some experienced violin teachers came to Matsumoto to study with him and observe his methods, and later to apply them in branches of Talent Education. Eventually some of his pupils became old enough to teach, first as assistants and then as regular branch teachers. Today he says that, as a rule, those who grew up learning by his method make better teachers of it than do the "converted" teachers. The system is of course more natural to those who themselves learned by it. There are now about one hundred teachers of Talent Education in some seventy-six branches throughout Japan. About 6,000 children are now studying violin in this way; how many "alumni" there are I do not know.

In 1955 the first Annual National Concert was given in Tokyo, with hundreds of children coming together from the various branches to perform their common repertoire. This spectacular affair attracted much attention.

In 1963, six weeks of visiting many branches of Saino-Kyoiku in Japan, (after my five years of correspondence with Mr. Suzuki which included tapes, pictures, programs, etc.) provided our present knowledge of this fascinating movement. So much for "historical background."

Mr. Suzuki will now speak for himself. Here are a few quotes from a 1963 speech, "Every Child Can Become Rich in Musical Sense."

Two facts that have become clear in these thirty years are: (1) if any child is brought up so that he hears good music (e.g., through records) every day from the time he is born, he will become a person with a rich musical sense; and (2) if any child is brought up so that he hears off-key, distorted music every day, the child will become tone-deaf.

Do not these findings tell us something important about the whole question of the hereditary transmission of human abilities and about the problem of education? If it is true that any child could be brought up to be tone-deaf, the universal belief that a talent for music is something certain children are born with would be merely an illusion. This has been my conclusion, and for years I have held that there is no such thing as an innate aptitude for music. I believe the same, of course, about other cultural skills. I have insisted that it is a mistake to think that hereditary aptitudes exist for literature, mathematics, or any such specific cultural activity . . .

How Ability Grows

The fact that ability does not develop without experience, for example, leads us to think about organisms and their environment. All who lived in the Stone Age grew up in the cultural environment of that time. Hence, even though there may have been innate differences among individuals, everyone remained at the Stone Age level in the development of their abilities.

However, the fact that abilities develop in response to environment opens up educational possibilities without limit. This is an important fact, because it means that if a child born today were brought up in a society five thousand years more advanced than ours, it could grow up into a person with the abilities of people five thousand years in the future.

My observations have led me to conclude that: Ability develops as a function of the effort of the life force to maintain itself—to survive by adjusting itself to its environment. I believe that in the field of education we must not forget that ability does not grow where there is no experience.

What Are Innate Individual Differences?

. . . Differences in ability to respond to the environment constitute differences in innate ability. . . . We could say that an individual who possesses the capacity to respond quicker and more sensitively than another to his environment is an innately superior being.

Fostering Musical Sense

In various parts of Japan today, there are members of our Association who are bringing up their babies on music, letting them listen every day to good music on record players.

A masterpiece by Bach, Mozart or Schubert, for example, is selected and the one selection is played every day for the baby. If the record is played every time the baby starts to cry, it will eventually reach the point where it will become quiet the moment the music begins and will listen attentively. Only the one selection must be used.

After about five months, any baby thus exposed will clearly learn the selection. There are some babies that have been brought up listening to a concerto (one movement only) by Bach or Vivaldi and have learned the music well. After about five months, another selection is added. The baby hears two selections every day. In this way, any baby will grow into a child with a rich musical sense. In other words, the environment develops a person's ability and senses.

In order to produce a tone-deaf child, a record of off-key, distorted music could be made and played daily from the time the baby is born. Since there has been no family thus far that has requested such an experiment with their baby, we have not tested this idea. However, without carrying out such an experiment, we already know some parents who have been raising their babies by singing lullabies out of tune every day and have fostered tone-deaf children, thus providing evidence for our purpose.

The method described above has its parallel in the development of a child's ability in its own native language in every country in the world. In any country, there are delicate differences of language native to the locality, and every child acquires completely the subtle differences of intonation and pronunciation of its locality. Life creates ability. And the type of education that focuses on the marvelous power of children to grow in ability is the best type of education.

Talent Education

. . .The development of ability in one's native language is, I believe, the best type of education in existence. It is in the conditions making up this kind of education that the best educational method can be found, for all children throughout the world have successfully grown up in this field of spoken language.

Talent Education merely applies the method of learning one's native language to education in music or some other subjects.

Education Through Living Situations

The first point to learn from the child's education in his native language is the fact that, from very simple beginnings, each item is applied in daily living situations until he fully absorbs it. In my educational method this is a primary point to which I strictly adhere . . . .

The idea is to add one new item at a time. Because training in one's native language takes place by this system, every child thoroughly absorbs the language. When the selections are learned so thoroughly that they are part of the child, then the ability that has been fostered to this stage becomes a powerful capacity that can be applied to learning the next new selection. The child therefore does not feel it particularly difficult but readily develops both his ability and his playing of a new selection.

The record player is the teacher in the home. The selection is played on the record over and over again until the tune is learned well beforehand, and then the child is taught to play it.

The children are instructed to be able to play at any time any of the many selections they have learned. This is the system of native language training. Children who have been taught in this manner from the beginning are able to perform easily.

The three important aspects of music education are (1) fostering musical sense, (2) developing performing ability, and (3) developing behavior and the mind (character). We keep these three aspects always in mind, placing emphasis on education in the home and developing the child in cooperation with the parents to become a good person.

For the Sake of All Children

When parents unwittingly raise their children to be tone-deaf in the home, or when children grow up without their ability being developed because their parents have done nothing about it, the music educator who has them put into his hands finds only a frustrating struggle to try to train them, for no matter how hard he may try, the children remain as the tragic products of mistaken upbringing. I am struck deeply by the misfortune of these children, all of whom were born with the wonderful capacity of showing the same type of ability as they show in their own native tongue.

I hope that an age will be created in our countries when babies are brought up listening to good music in every home, so that all children will be rich in musical sense. The cooperation of record firms will be needed.

This should be a primary national policy, in making music education succeed. Casals said: 'Music will save the world!' This will happen if we exert our efforts towards this end.

I am deeply grateful to be counted as one of those who know that music has an invisible but mighty living power to save mankind.

Now let us consider some details of the method. *Listening* is the first step—listening to a record *at home*, and to the teacher and other children playing the same music. After the first piece is firmly established in the ear and the child, perhaps three or four years old, has learned to hold violin and bow, brief lessons for child *and* mother start to show what to do to produce the sounds already in the ear. The mother continues work with the child at home. Each number is learned thoroughly and is reviewed and kept up. The child reads no printed music at all, but the mother may need the printed music to refer to—to check a fingering or other detail. Volume I starts with a set of variations on "Twinkle, Twinkle, Little Star" and progresses through plateaus* through folksongs and other little pieces, then come three Bach "Menuets" and finally a Gossec "Gavotte."

In most branches the children come together once a month or so to play with each other, they do "games" or "tests," and hear each other play. These classes are very instructive and valuable. It was a great pleasure to watch Mr. Suzuki conduct many of them.

Volume IV of the method contains the Vivaldi Concerto in A minor; this is the stage where reading and vibrato begin in most cases, with notation gradually presented as a "picture" of what has already been played. But even when the printed page is used, ear work is continued. The final Volumes, IX and X, consist of the Mozart Concertos Nos. 4 and 5. A wide range of repertoire is played after completion of the volumes of the method. At private lessons with

---

*For a description of one plateau, see page 75.

advanced students, Mr. Suzuki constantly referred to himself as "assistant" to Kreisler, Grumiaux, Neveu, or other top artists whose recording the student was using as a model. Suzuki was thus free to devote his lessons to tone and finesse. His ear for sound (not just pitch) is fabulous. He says: "Tone has soul without body."

Of course the children progress at different rates of speed. Here are a few sample performances I heard: Hitomi Kasuya, four and a half ("doll girl"—given a violin to play with instead of a doll), first movement of Vivaldi Concerto; Asako Hata, seven, all of Bach A minor Concerto; Yukari Tate, thirteen, Chausson "Poème"; Eiko Suzuki, sixteen, Tchaikovsky "Concerto," Bach Suite in D minor; Tomiko Shida, twenty-one, artist recital, First Prize Brussels Conservatory, winner of a Munich international violin competition. These names are only a few out of hundreds who played well!

I do not wish to reiterate what has already been written about Talent Education or to start on the myriad of details concerning the organization, its very interesting advisors, its system of intercommunication and yearly schedule of performances and meetings. I prefer now to give some insights into the thinking and actions of the remarkable man who is the guiding genius of Talent Education.

He speaks much of "heart" in music and puts it first in importance, with the musical factor second, and the technical part third. Mild-mannered as he is, he is severely critical of any violinist (no matter how celebrated) whose playing lacks warmth and humanity.

He has many clever little tricks for speeding up students' reactions, for securing relaxation and concentration, and for testing security and knowledge. For example, if a child cannot answer a question while playing a piece, without missing a note, he is told "More work! You don't know it yet!" Or a group may be divided into halves to play a concerto. One half starts playing—at a clap from the teacher the other half must pick it up without missing a beat or note. This alternation goes on throughout the selection.

Mrs Suzuki told me privately that he believes he has the "power of healing" in his hands. He certainly has the power of getting quick improvement from his students. A true mystic and believer, he is not interested in money or possessions. He is often taken advantage of by unscrupulous people. His interest in the unfortunate or handicapped is unfailing; for example, consider his attention and help for Kiyoshi Yamashita, now forty-one, an artist—imbecile with an IQ of 30–40. All he can do is draw and paint, but instead of rotting in an institution he has been aided in doing what he can by what may be called a form of "Talent Education." Nothing challenges Mr. Suzuki more than an unlikely prospect for learning the violin. One of his pupils was extremely slow and considered to be "tone-deaf." She now can do a reasonable job on the Brahms "Concerto." Mr. Suzuki looks like a cat which has just swallowed a mouse when he says "Good example!"

He freely admits his own limitations, but says they do not apply to his young students. "I do what I can," he says—not a bad philosophy! One of his tests consisted of having two young students memorize a complete Vivaldi "Double Concerto" and play it for an NHK* recording—*all in one day!* "They could do it; I couldn't," he says. Progress in music comes by students' excelling their teachers.

Once on the way to a concert where a child was to play Chausson's "Poème" he found she was "anxious." "Play for Chausson, not publicum. If you play for publicum you

---

*The Japanese government broadcasting system.

are same as Geisha girl." He says contests are often more
for teachers than students.

In one group performance he removed a child who
couldn't play his part. When the father demanded "What's
the matter?" Mr. Suzuki wasted no time in replying "*You!*"
Parents *are* responsible for their children.

He never tires of preaching on his favorite subjects, "The
Happiness of All Children," and "Save the World by Music."

One final quotation from Mr. Suzuki: "All growth begins from the day of birth. If the seedling is spoiled, nothing
can be done about the sad fate of that plant or being.
Abilities develop only for things which have been experienced. The fate of a child is in the hands of his parents.
Every child has been born with high potentialities. The
greatest duty and joy given to us adults is the privilege of
developing these potentialities and of educating desirable
human beings with beautiful, harmonious minds and high
sensitivity. The day will come when all children in the world
will be educated and trained to be happy human beings.
When I think of man's essential readiness to develop into
any type of person in accordance with his environment, I am
strongly impressed with the great love and blessings show-
ered by Nature upon mankind."

Mr. Suzuki is truly one of the most fascinating persons I
have ever met!

Chapter V

Talent Education Comes to the States

As noted in Chapter I, I had written in 1959: "Perhaps Mr. Suzuki and a representative number of Japanese youngsters might appear at one of our national meetings?" This hope was fulfilled by the first American tour, made in March of 1964.

The Philadelphia Story

On March 15th, Mr. Suzuki and a group of his young Japanese violinists made a sensational appearance in Philadelphia at a joint session of the American String Teachers Association and the Music Educators National Conference. John Kendall and I were Co-Chairmen. After the children had played their program I read my "Summary" which makes up Chapter III of this book. I also made several remarks which are now repeated.

In answer to the question in everyone's mind after hearing the children play—"There are plenty more children like these in Japan!"

"Talent Education, or *musical education,* is literally a cradle-to-grave (or 'womb-to-tomb') proposition—the worthwhile kind of education. Great emphasis is placed on improving education today, especially *higher education.* Frankly, I'm more impressed with what Mr. Suzuki is doing than by the fact that the University of 'X' has flunked out 2,000 students this quarter. The place to start improving education of any kind is at the beginning, not at the end!"

Mr. Suzuki had prepared a pamphlet, "Every Child Can Be Educated," for distribution in Philadelphia. Unfortunately, it arrived in the States too late. Here is most of the text:

Ladies and gentlemen, I sincerely urge you to take steps towards a revolution in musical education for the sake of the happiness of each and every child in the United States. I wish to encourage you all to explore and develop the means by which all children can be educated to make full use of their abilities.

Not only in music, but in many other fields as well, children are often educated in a way which stunts and damages their abilities. It is my belief that attention should be given to a child's education from the day of his birth. Educators are often presented with pupils whose correct education has been neglected, whose abilities have been impaired, and who have been turned into pitifully stunted, thwarted children. When confronted with such pupils, educators in the past were often inclined to think that such children were born with innately inferior abilities. Today, the time has come when we must reject this attitude as an erroneous one. Every child, except a baby one day old, is what he is because of what he has been taught. The abilities displayed by any child are the results of the training which he has been given in the past.

In considering the inborn nature of human beings, we ought, I think, to give deep thought to the nature of a baby on the day of its birth.

One day about thirty years ago, I made a discovery which overwhelmed me with astonishment. I discovered at that time that all children throughout the world are educated to speak their native languages with the utmost fluency. This education in their native languages enables them to develop their linguistic abilities successfully to an extremely high level. This discovery made me realize that any child will be able to display highly superior abilities if only the correct methods are used in training and developing these abilities.

Is this not an astonishing fact? All children everywhere in the world are educated by a method which has been in continuous practice throughout all human history. A child's abilities develop by being developed.

The method of education which I have been using thus far

is nothing but this method of education in the native language applied without any essential modifications to musical education.

Today, I should like to report to you concerning two principles which I regard as the most important elements in this method of education which I have been using.

The first principle concerns musical education for developing an ear for music.

In the past, it was generally believed that an ear for music was something innate. However, this idea is an error. An ear for music is something which has to be acquired by listening, and the sooner this is begun the more effective it will be. However, it is evident that an ear for music is not innate. My thirty years of experience have taught me clearly that this is so. An ear for music is a human aptitude which can only be developed by listening.

I invite you to try it. Select one piece of great music for a newborn baby. Train the baby by letting him listen every day to a record or a tape recording of this same piece of music.

The baby is made to listen to only one piece repeatedly. If this is done, it will be found that any baby, after five or six months, will have clearly memorized the piece of music.* If the child is brought up day after day in this atmosphere of good music, there can be no doubt that the child will eventually grow up into a young person with an excellent ear for music. This experiment has already been carried out successfully by hundreds of families.

By the same token, if a baby is brought up listening day after day to a melody played off-key by a tone-deaf person (it is a necessary condition that the baby should be made to listen to the same piece repeatedly), then any baby brought up under such conditions will grow up tone-deaf. Examples of this may be found everywhere in families where the parents are tone-deaf.

The day is already past when music education regarded an ear for music as something innate and when it was not considered necessary to train it. I invite all of you to prove this experimentally. In short, this means that there is no such thing as an innate aptitude for music.

Instead of this, I regard the following as the basic principle governing the development of human abilities:

"Abilities are born and developed by the workings of the

---

*See Suzuki's book, *Nurtured by Love*, p. 17.

vital forces of the organism as it strives to live and to adjust to its environment."

Of course, there are individuals who are born with inherently superior or inferior qualities, and differences in ability no doubt occur because of these innate differences. However, it is my belief that innate superiority or inferiority is basically nothing but a relatively superior or inferior ability to adjust to environmental conditions.

On the basis of these ideas and of the results of my work for the past thirty years, one of the educational methods which I should like to recommend to you is the following:

Education for the development of an ear for music should form a part of all musical education, whether private teaching or musical instruction in the school. The methodology which I recommend is the following. The piece which is to be learned should always be played beforehand to the pupils every day by means of records or tape recordings in order to develop their ear for music. The pupils should also continue to listen to the records or tapes while they are learning the piece. Of course, in order to carry out this method, it is essential to have records or tape recordings of superior performances of the music. This method is employed, not in order to familiarize the pupils with new pieces, but rather to develop an ear for music in each child. It may safely be predicted that the ear for music will develop in direct proportion to the number of times the piece is heard by the pupils. This method will be equally effective if the music is played in the room while the pupils are studying another subject, for instance arithmetic. As long as the music is audible, the life forces of the human being will unconsciously absorb it, making it a part of the individual's abilities.

I have followed this method faithfully thus far, and I have been quite amazed at how wonderfully the children's ear for music has developed.

I feel strongly that education aimed at developing the ear for music is undoubtedly the most important element in musical education, and I am sure that the day will come when this method will be accepted as a matter of common sense in musical education all over the world. It cannot be otherwise, for the results have been revealed only too obviously.

However, one must not expect far-reaching results after only a short period during which the pupils listen to only small amounts of music. Such expectations would be doomed to disappointment. Musical sense develops gradually and imperceptibly,

just as linguistic sense does. The same thing is true of the learning of speech patterns by American children. Children who grow
up in Boston will by an imperceptible process become speakers
of American English with a distinctive Bostonian melody, while
those who grow up in New York will also gradually become
speakers of New York English. This is so because of the conditions under which the "ear for language" develops. The same
conditions apply also to the development of the ear for music.

The second principle in musical education is the need for
attaining thorough mastery.

This is one of the most important elements in developing
performing techniques. It also is a method which comes from
the methods of learning the native language.

The principle is this: "From the very beginning, every step
must by all means be thoroughly mastered."

This is an important principle in education for the purpose
of developing the abilities.

There are some teachers who go on immediately from one
piece to the next as soon as the pupil has learned how to play.
I am sure that all of you know of many examples of pupils of
such teachers who have turned out as failures. This system results in failure because it concentrates merely on increasing the
number of pieces learned, rather than on developing ability,
which is what is really important. Failures of this type are especially frequent in beginners who have not yet attained the
necessary ability.

There is a certain period when the pupil has finally become
able to play his first piece. I call this period the time when the
pupil is "prepared." I tell the pupil: "Now the lessons will really
begin. From now on, your abilities will begin to develop." From
this point, I start to train the pupil, and I continue this until
he has attained thorough mastery.

For instance, let us suppose that the pupil has become able
to play piece A well. At this time, I will add piece B. We will
then work on piece B while still continuing to work on piece A.
The lessons will include both piece A and piece B. As soon as
the pupil can play piece B quite well, I will add piece C to
pieces A and B. When finally piece D has been added to the
lessons, the emphasis on piece A will be reduced, and the lessons
will consist of pieces B, C, and D. This is the method by which
I instruct beginners.

By this means, while new pieces are added, emphasis is laid

on increasing the ability to play the pieces already learned, thus increasing little by little the performing skill.

In this way, regular sequence is followed, and the ability is developed to play all of the pieces which have been learned, pieces A, B, C, and D. As the abilities are developed gradually in this way, the skills accumulated will add up to an ever-increasing store of basic ability making possible further great advances in ability.

I feel strongly that every child attains the superior ability to speak American English fluently and skillfully precisely because this method of education is adopted in teaching speech habits. The above method of attaining thorough mastery is the second method which I wish to suggest to you.

I sincerely urge you to conduct a mighty educational movement to develop an ear for music in all American children. Today when we have records and tapes, this method of education may be carried out anywhere. However, the most important thing of all is to conduct a social movement to encourage parents in the home to give their children an ear for music from the time when they are still babies. If only this practice were to become a matter accepted as common sense in all families in society in general, it would undoubtedly resolve our difficulties in music education in the school. If only this were done, children would come to school with a well-developed ear for music, and wonderful results could be attained in music education.

How is it possible for us to give musical education to children who have been made tone-deaf in their homes? Musical aptitude is not inborn.

Let us work together to bring about an age of a new human race. Ladies and gentlemen, I urge you to explore and develop new paths for the education of children so that all American children will be given the happiness which they deserve.

The Oberlin Story

The cover picture on the *Oberlin Alumni Magazine* of May, 1964, was described thus: "Eric Moore, four-year-old son of DeVere E. Moore, associate professor of woodwinds, plays with Hitomi Kasuya, 5-year-old Japanese, as the troup of ten tiny Japanese children and their teacher, Shinichi

Suzuki, delighted and astounded Oberlin audiences on March 16." The magazine contained my article, "Genius by the Gross;" the following are a few quotes:

A very pleasant dream came true for me on March 16th, 1964, when Mr. Shinichi Suzuki and ten child violinists from Japan, aged 5 to 14 years, gave two memorable concerts in Oberlin's Warner Hall. These demonstration-recitals were the culmination of a relationship between Mr. Suzuki and me which began in 1958. . . . Interest in Mr. Suzuki's work has since spread throughout the United States . . .

Last fall Miss Hiroko Yamada, former student of Mr. Suzuki in Matsumoto and now a special student in the Conservatory, and I started about 30 children from the Oberlin area in learning to play violin by the Talent Education system. Most of these children are from 3 to 6 years of age, and they use tiny 16th, 10th, 8th, or quarter-size violins. Short individual lessons have been given the children and their mothers (or fathers) once a week; two epidemics of measles, flu, scarlet fever and other childhood diseases caused numerous absences. One mother now says of her 4-year-old violinist, "He can't blow his nose yet, but he *can* play Twinkle, Twinkle Variations!"

A coast-to-coast tour of the States for Suzuki and the ten Japanese children was arranged for March by a committee consisting of Professor John Kendall of Southern Illinois University, Dr. Robert Klotman of Detroit, President of the American String Teachers Association, and myself. This highly successful tour included performances at many universities, music schools, state and national conventions of music teachers, the United Nations, and several television appearances. The children created a sensation wherever they played.

What a pleasure it was to have them play with our children in an afternoon session in Warner Concert Hall! (Our children and their parents are still talking about it.) In the evening Mr. Suzuki and his young violinists appeared before a packed audience in group performances, games, solos, and an explanation of his method for developing children's character at an early age through music study. The children were literally the "talk of the town" and many visitors came from other parts of Ohio to hear them. A question-answer period followed the program.

At about the same time Scherl & Roth published a short article of mine, "Suzuki in Oberlin." Here is a portion of the article:

. . . Our problem of securing small-size violins was solved through Heinrich Roth's help, and around the first of November, we started. Because of our own time limitations, we could meet with the children only once a week. We soon found that for young preschool children, a short private lesson with only the mother and/or other family member present was the most effective teaching approach. After several lessons, the children enjoy getting together at times to play with—and for—each other.

One of the greatest difficulties in starting a program is that it is not possible to present the inspiring example of more advanced children's playing. Playing by teachers and adults does not provide the same motivation as that afforded by children's playing. However, Mr. Suzuki says the beginning is always very slow; it took him about five years to get his own program well under way.

Basic to the method is listening to high-quality performances on record or tape. *The "model" must, of course, be the finest obtainable.* A very early start at training the ear is essential; and actual instruction on the violin usually begins at about age three. The short attention-span of such youngsters calls for very short lessons and much patience on the part of teachers and parents. It is essential to have proper cooperation from the parent who attends the lesson—in providing good home environment and seeing that regular homework is done.

Absolutely fundamental in the method is mastery of each step before moving on to the next. This very slow beginning irks many American parents who expect a new piece each week and tend to measure progress by quantity rather than quality. When he encounters such an attitude, Mr. Suzuki's very effective deflating question is, 'And where are you hurrying?'

It was a tremendous advantage for our parents and children to hear the Japanese children in Oberlin. Thus inspired, our children are really "catching on." Many are successfully completing the necessarily-slow beginning stages and are ready to move. Our experience with these children so far has convinced me of the tremendous possibilities opened up for us by the modest, enthusiatic violin teacher from Japan!

Chapter VI

Preparing for Workshop

Mr. Suzuki agreed to conduct several workshops for teachers and students in the States, to be held in the summer of 1965. In the spring of that year I wrote several articles as publicity preparation for our workshop. This chapter includes a few quotes from these articles.

My grandson, Jeffrey Lancashire, is two years old and all boy. He plays with trucks, tractors, trains and other typical boy toys. But when he sees a violinist preparing to play on TV he becomes quite excited, claps and sings "Twinkle, Twinkle, Little Star." Why? It's quite a story.

Our sixth College-Community String Festival was held in Finney Chapel on January 16, 1965. The concert opened with a group of selections played by thirty young violinists from the Oberlin Suzuki Class. (The Misses Hiroko Yamada and Hiroko Toba, Suzuki students for many years and teachers for him in Matsumoto, now teach more than forty children from the Oberlin area.) The violin sections of the large Festival String Orchestra which played Ernest Bloch's Concerto Grosso No. 1 included, beside the two Hirokos, two more young Japanese women students in the Conservatory.

Jenny Lancashire, my 3-year-old granddaughter, played the first variation of "Twinkle, Twinkle" in this concert. Her two-year-old brother, Jeff, has heard her practicing and playing the model record she listens to. When he reaches the ripe old age of three he will be well prepared to start his study on her 1/10 size violin. Here ends the story of Jeff—for the present.

Mr. Suzuki's connection with Oberlin will be continued this summer. From June 24 to July 17 he will be teaching our children, demonstrating and lecturing for visiting teachers. The Oberlin College Conservatory of Music is providing this unique, extended opportunity for music teachers to learn in depth Suzuki's ideas and see them applied to children.*

Addendum, 1969

Jeff did start violin at three, but his interest in other fields remained stronger. The high point in his career as a violinist came at one of our public concerts. He reluctantly came out on the stage with the children when his level was reached, but I saw that he intended to jump off the stage and go back down into the audience. A four-foot jump might well break his violin, I thought frantically!

Very quickly I sat on the front edge of the stage and pulled him down beside me. Together, with our feet hanging toward the floor, we played our violins in the Variations. Our performance attracted attention and caused laughter—a good example of the many unexpected things that happen at concerts given by children.

Jenny is now studying with Kazuko Numanami, as this is written. But Erica Morini is safe!

Violin study is begun at a very early age by the Suzuki students, after a period of listening to records of fine music performed by artists. *Three is probably the most common age for starting on a Japanese 1/10 size violin.* Music is learned by ear, not by eye, up to the level of a Vivaldi concerto in most cases. Even in more advanced study, the ear is emphasized and recordings and tapes are important adjuncts to the lessons.

How efficient the method is may be judged by the performances of the ten Japanese children in this country last March. (Pictured with Mr. Suzuki is Yukari Tate, 14 years old, who played Chausson's "Poème" like an artist.) The writer heard hundreds of fine performances in Japan during his visit with Mr. Suzuki and other Talent Education teachers in many centers.

An interesting feature of the new Oberlin Conservatory com-

---

*From "Oberlin College Imports the Suzuki Method" in *Fine Arts,* April 11, 1965.

plex of buildings is their resemblance to a Japanese inn, or
ryokan. Architect Minoru Yamasaki has arranged the buildings
so there is an attractive view of a garden-like spot from every
room. The central garden, with its reflecting pool, stones, and
small pine trees is typically Japanese. Mr. Suzuki will appear
at home in this setting and he will have much to offer the
students and teachers who are fortunate enough to attend his
sessions.*

---

*From "Suzuki in Oberlin" in the *Music Educators Journal,* April-May
1965.

Chapter VII

*Suzuki Workshop**

Instead of the usual three-ring circus type of workshop, the Suzuki Workshop for the teaching of violin, held from June 25 to July 17, was geared to a single purpose. It provided, in depth, an opportunity for teachers to become acquainted with the thinking and the violin teaching of Shinichi Suzuki, and thereby to eradicate, as much as possible, the common misconceptions on this subject. With its quiet, unhurried atmosphere and lack of distractions, Oberlin in summertime proved an ideal location for such a workshop. From 9 to 11 every morning Mr. Suzuki gave lessons in the new Kulas Recital Hall, and from 11:15-12:30 he lectured, demonstrated, and led the teachers, who had their violins in hand. Mrs. Suzuki and Miss Yuko Honda assisted him. Some afternoons were filled with playing sessions for teachers, private lessons, movies or slides, string orchestra or ensembles. But there was also ample time provided for the teachers to use the practice facilities in Robertson Hall.

About one hundred twenty teachers attended the workshop, from twenty-six states and four Canadian provinces. They included college, conservatory, public-school and private teachers, and professional players. Some thirty-five students, ranging from three-year-olds to teachers and professionals, had individual public lessons with Mr. Suzuki on the stage of Kulas Hall while the others observed. Some

---

*Reprinted from the *Oberlin Alumni Magazine* of December, 1965.

seventeen more had private lessons with him. Mr. Suzuki also held short group lessons with children from Oberlin, Yellow Springs, and Put-in-Bay. During his stay Mr. Suzuki taught for one afternoon at Antioch College and lectured once at Western Reserve University.

Typical of the comments of many of the teachers attending the Workshop was the following: "These were the best two weeks of my life." Such comments more than repaid the considerable effort involved in preparing and operating the Workshop.

Interpreters find Suzuki difficult to work with because he likes to coin phrases with his own special meaning: "Soft iron," "Frog tone," "Strike!" (when a boy plays a passage exactly right); "Important nothing" (the gap between staccato tones); "Antenna" (bow upright on top of a child's head); "Up-bow natural for babies" (they work everything *up* to their mouths); "Please open door before entering," "Nice face important in playing," "We don't play the piano sideways, and piano doesn't move around while being played"; "Your tone is *glass*" (after a lecture on the difference between diamond and glass); "Don't make accessories bigger than people"; "Kreisler highway" (part of string between bridge and circle of F hole). A steady stream of comments like these keeps his teaching fast and sharp, alert and vital.

He brings down the house when he demonstrates the way a student would learn to walk if the student's current bowing method were used; or when he rests a student's bow on the piano lid and bends over to watch it closely after the student tells him that the bow "springs." He advises, "Don't hunt for something on the floor," with appropriate mimicry, when he is teaching a student how to bow (bough). He finds a child's nose useful—to turn the child's head, lead him, or to measure bowing: "Use bow stroke as wide as your nose."

His strong will to improve is a dominating force. He plays a recording of the finest performance he can find as a model for his students and then says: "A record is stopped, cannot grow. We must always grow—*higher!* Students must become better than their teachers or we go back to the Stone Age."

"Education" in Japanese is two words: *Kyo* (Teach) and *Iku* (Growth). Mr. Suzuki thinks there is more teaching, usually, than growth. Preparation, he believes, should come first; then *Kyo*, then *Iku, Iku, Iku.* The common procedure in schools is, he feels: teach, examine, teach, examine. He advocates teaching after examinations, not just before. "Most examinations," he says, "are for teachers, not pupils. We *know* so much, but *do* so little—like a library. We must *do* something! Others are influenced by what we *do*, not what we say." He emphasizes the importance of a good heart, a good attitude. He once sent a student to play the Bach "Chaconne" in an empty church—"to God." His final test for those he is preparing to be teachers is that they be considerate and thoughtful of others, not interested solely in the violin and in themselves. Then they are ready to teach.

The Workshop came to a close on a Saturday noon, with all the teachers playing "Auld Lang Syne" and Mr. Suzuki thanking them by playing the "Nagoya Lullaby." The first summer workshop in the New Conservatory Complex was over.*

RÉSUMÉ OF THE SUZUKI SEMINAR†
(held at Oberlin College, June 25–July 17, 1965)

---

*(Subsequent workshops, held in Oberlin and elsewhere, are noted in Chapter XIV.)

†This résumé, dated July 15, 1965, was prepared by a committee of string teachers attending the seminar.

The Talent Education program, as formulated and presented to us by Mr. Shinichi Suzuki, is concerned with the development of the potential in all children to a much higher level, much earlier than has been previously attempted. Those of us who are violinists are naturally concerned principally with Mr. Suzuki's approach to the teaching of the instrument, although it cannot really be divorced from the training of the child as a human being.

To be a good violinist, a child must have an adequate grounding in ear-training, in technical achievement and in musicianship. We believe the Suzuki method to be outstanding in all three aspects, particularly in ear-training, which is the basis for both technical excellence and musicianship. Every step along the way is so carefully planned and well presented that the foundation of a superior technique is solidly laid.

We were greatly impressed by the constant emphasis on listening to each tone produced, constantly endeavoring to improve tone quality. The plucking of the string, both open and fingered, hearing the resonance and then matching with the bowed stroke the same clear attack and balanced release (thereby permitting the string to "echo") we believe to be an excellent method to develop an ear for tone quality, and also to develop a strong left hand.

Throughout the seminar the accent was on balance—of body, of violin, and especially of the bow arm. To achieve this balance or "weightlessness" Mr. Suzuki constantly pointed out the action of the thumb and first fingers and, above all, of the whole arm moving naturally. From the time the child holds his bow for the first time, he is given exercises to develop a balanced bow arm. One which we thought to be of particular value was the vertical oscillation of the bow, tip and frog moving the same distance, propelled by the entire arm. This exercise strengthens and vitalizes the fingers of the bow hand, as well as causing the entire arm to move vigorously as a unit. Another exercise he uses from the very beginning requires the bow to be held upright and the point allowed to move in a small arc, propelled only by the fingers. This develops both strength and mobility of the hand and fingers.

If we were to look for key words to describe Mr. Suzuki's method, they would probably be "listen," "imitate," and "balance." The child listens to the record, to his teacher, to his own tone, constantly tries to imitate the best and to achieve balance in his own playing.

We were also interested in the fact that he has children begin with a very small amount of bow, in contrast to methods which stress early use of the entire bow. Thus the bowing from the very beginning is alive and vital, with much less chance of developing the "slip tone."

We have concluded, along with Mr. Suzuki, that this is not basically a group method. Playing in groups is important to the child's growth, but the teaching needs to be done individually, both because it requires careful listening to the child's own tone and because each child progresses at a different rate. Mr. Suzuki stresses the fact that *every* child, given the proper environment, can learn to play the violin. Some children will go much faster than others; some will eventually become more outstanding violinists than others; but each child can learn to play, and to play well, at whatever level he may reach.

Mr. Suzuki has presented us with a method that not only ought to work, but incontrovertibly *does* work, as those of us who heard the children who came with him to this country a year ago can testify. Whether it can work equally well in America only time will tell, but we believe that results here will bear out the faith we have in this method. We are not sure that American mothers have the time or patience to do what Japanese mothers do to augment the work of the teacher, but maybe we underestimate the Americans. We are not sure that the climate of the home, or the relationship of pupil to teacher, both essential to the success of the method in Japan, can be duplicated in America. Again, only time will tell, but we believe that, with minor adjustments, results will be just as satisfying here as in Japan.

It was a great joy for us to watch Mr. Suzuki working with the children whose lessons we observed. In this relationship of teacher with pupil lies not only the secret of a great teacher of the violin, but also of a great-hearted man. We are all a little better, both as teachers and as human beings, for having had this privilege. We wish him continued success with his work in Japan, and thank him for sharing himself with us for these three weeks.

Chapter VIII

Tenth Anniversary Celebration

The program for the 1968 tour of Japanese children contained my short article, "A Memorable 10th Anniversary." Here is a condensation:

Ten years ago Kenji Mochizuki was a Japanese student in the Graduate School of Theology of Oberlin College. His interest in both religious and musical education was to produce a very practical and significant result. . . .

What changes have taken place in the States in these last ten years! Thousands of Americans now know of Dr. Suzuki and his Talent Education . . . through hearing his children play on their transcontinental tours . . . through attending his coast-to-coast workshops or from trips to Japan . . . through reading some of the many articles written about his work . . . and through hearing our American children play in the numerous centers where experimentation with the Suzuki Method is now in progress.

It is even possible to reminisce a bit about the movement in America. How grateful I was to Heinrich Roth for helping to get the small instruments needed to start our program, after many firms had offered only discouragement! What a problem getting the books and records has been until now! How much I've learned from the playing, teaching, and conversation of the five young graduates Mr. Suzuki has sent to teach at Oberlin through the years! How convincing the "proof of the pudding" has been in Japan! How important that we pass the test of *producing* more than hot air here in the States! And finally, what a debt we owe to our little Japanese friend with the big ideas and the big heart—Suzuki!

Today Kenji Mochizuki is an official at the Consulate General of Japan in New York. As he returns to Oberlin in October of 1968 with the touring Suzuki children, we plan a fitting celebration for the tenth year since we first saw and heard the Tokyo film of the Bach Double Concerto. It will be a happy occasion.

The *Oberlin Alumni Magazine,* January, 1969, included
an article, "Suzuki Anniversary," written by the editor, Philip
F. Tear. Some quotes are:

To mark the anniversary, 11 Japanese children—aged 5 to 18
—gave workshops and concerts in Oberlin Oct. 20-21 during a
nationwide Talent Education tour. Featured in the programs
were Yukari Tate, 18, who made her debut at Carnegie Recital
Hall in November, and Hitomi Kasuya, 9, a soloist who demonstrated Suzuki's Talent Education method.

Coming at the close of Homecoming Weekend, the Suzuki
anniversary celebration gave alumni an opportunity to watch the
workshop in Warner Concert Hall Oct. 20 when Oberlin children
enrolled in Suzuki classes joined the Japanese children on stage.

Mochizuki returned to Oberlin with the touring children. In
addition to his duties at the consulate, he served as tour director
for the 1966, 1967 and 1968 U.S.A. tours of Suzuki children. . . .

"Small children develop their abilities far beyond what their
parents or the world expect of them," says Suzuki. "As long as
they have a normal mental ability to learn, any child can be
taught to appreciate music." The Suzuki method does not teach
children to become professional musicians, but more than 100 of
Japan's professional violinists have come out of the Suzuki school.

Oberlin's Suzuki-type program, established in 1963, is showing similar success as are the programs started more recently at
the New England Conservatory of Music and at Eastman School.

Now the cello has been added to the method. Two examples
were offered at the workshop in Oberlin when Tomoyuki Nomura,
7, and Koji Yanagita, 13, performed. Playing together is a regular feature for Suzuki students.

Yukari Tate began her studies with Shinichi Suzuki when
she was three years old. At the age of nine, she graduated with
honor from the most advanced course at the Suzuki School. From
1960 to 1962, she traveled with Suzuki to various cities in Japan,
presenting demonstrations of his teaching method.

In March of 1964, when she was 14, she came to the United
States with other students of the Suzuki method and performed
at several conservatories and universities. She gave a solo performance of the Chausson "Poème," Op. 25, at the Music Educators
National Conference in Philadelphia. As a senior member of the
group of Suzuki students, she made transcontinental tours of the

United States and Canada in 1966 and 1967. (Her solo recital in Oberlin on October 21, 1968, was her U.S. debut recital. Suzuki writes of her: "For myself, I discern in her playing the reflection of an exalted spirit purified by the power of music.")

Hitomi Kasuya, of course, was no stranger to an Oberlin audience. She was one of 10 touring Suzuki pupils who astounded Oberlinians in March, 1964 when she was five years old. She was one of the children whose photo appeared on the cover of the May 1964 issue of the *Oberlin Alumni Magazine*. . . .

Since then the Conservatory has conducted summer workshops to explain the Suzuki method to music teachers from the U.S. and Canada. Shinichi Suzuki himself conducted the 1965 and 1967 workshops.

Several music critics reviewed our celebration. The article by Boris Nelson in the *Toledo Blade* of October 27, 1968, was captioned "Tots Imitate What They Hear, Do Wonders Under Suzuki." A few quotes follow:

"Fantastic!" exclaimed the lady next me.

"Fabulous!" echoed the gentleman in front of me.

"Incredible!" I managed myself.

All around, the sophisticated music students of Oberlin College sat with their mouths wide open and their eyes glued to the stage of Warner Hall. It was the occasion of the 10th anniversary of the introduction at Oberlin of the Suzuki's Talent Education approach to string education.

Ten youngsters, between the ages of 5 and 13, were performing music by Fiocco, Vivaldi, Bach, Mozart, Schumann, and Boccherini.

And incredible it was indeed, as the youngsters, dead serious and as one with their instruments—one-half, one-quarter, one-eighth, one-tenth, and one-sixteenth their regular sizes—played with a technical proficiency, a musical sense, a surety of pitch, a virility of tone and the most sensitive phrasing that belied their age, their stumbling onto stage, their cutting up when they were not making music. . . .

Watching one of Suzuki's disciple-teachers, Mitsumasa Denda, instruct a stage full of American small fry in a workshop was an experience to be envied.

How to hold the violin becomes a game, the balancing of the bow a challenge, the use of the open strings permits holding hands with your partner. The immediate pleasure of producing not only sound but a recognizable tune is amazingly satisfying.

This, then, is Talent Education: a total involvement by the child with an example, a model, and an even more total involvement by the teacher with the child.

Since 1946, when Suzuki started out with his new method, many thousands of Japanese children have studied under talent education.

"We are not teaching them to become professional musicians," writes Suzuki. "I believe sensitivity and love for music or art are very important to all people. These are things that enrich our lives."

And yet, professionals have emerged from Suzuki's teaching, as Toshiya Eto at the Curtis Institute; Koji Toyoda, concertmaster of the Berlin Radio Orchestra; Takeshi Kobayashi, concertmaster of the Czech Orchestra; Hiroko Yamada, with the Rotterdam Orchestra; Takuya Shida with the Amsterdam Concertgebow Orchestra; and, no less, 18-year-old Yukari Tate, graduate assistant to Mr. Suzuki, who will make her Carnegie Hall debut on Nov. 4.

If she plays her program as she did in the evening at Oberlin, then she is sure to be rated among the very top of today's violinists. Playing a Stradivarius-on-loan, comely Miss Tate played the first movement (Allegro Maestoso) of the Concerto No. 1 in D by Paganini and she played it with absolute technical surety, but also with great musical flair and meaning.

Of course, there is more to it. The affection between the 10 youngsters from Japan who performed such little miracles for their teachers was obvious, but so was their respect.

And the discipline and concentration, the devotion with which they tackled the music goes beyond the lesson and the method: it goes back to the home where there are not as many distractions in Japan as there are here, and where praise takes the place of reward, where practicing music is a privilege and not a chore.

These youngsters, we were assured, were not specially gifted. To be sure, they had been in the program for some time, even the 5- and 6-year-old ones, but they were picked geographically and from different teachers, but within the same method.

More recently, the cello was added to the violin's method. Two examples were offered when 7-year-old Tomoyuki Nomura and 13-year-old Koji Yanagita performed, the latter the first movement from Boccherini's Cello Concerto in B-flat. It was cello playing of the very first order—security of fingering, but much more important, a feeling for the music, the line, the phrase.

This was perhaps even more astonishing than the technical end of all this music making, the sense for music. . . .

Several prominent American music educators have formed a group to push this program here at home. Surprisingly enough, these teachers are enthusiastic about their new-found work and they use the European class method as if born to it.

How fascinating it was Sunday to see these youngsters, now on a month's exhibition tour throughout the United States, play together, and I mean absolutely together, without a conductor. Or their complete knowledge of the music of the Double Concerto for Violin by Bach. Eight violins were involved during the workshop and as their mentor arbitrarily changed their positions, they switched parts, now first, now second. And without hesitation, they knew where they were and played on.

"Tiny Japanese Violinists Astonish" was Theodore Price's article in the *Akron Beacon Journal*, October 21, 1968. Here are excerpts:

. . . Little Kumiko Kitazawa, 5, played a captivating "Loure" by Bach on her small size violin. Koji Yanagita, 13, gave a supple, well-balanced performance of the first movement of Boccherini's Concerto in B-flat for cello.

When the group played together, everything about these young string whizzes was a kind of musical miracle. Six little girls in white dresses, and four boys in dark suits, playing together with incredible accuracy and flair—how do they do it?

Well, they started early. And I mean "early." . . . Conditioning, simple conditioning. And plenty of practice.

Eighteen-year-old Yukari Tate was guest soloist on this phenomenal concert. She played the Allegro Maestoso from Paganini's Violin Concerto in D with fluency and fire, as well as technical ease, dynamic control and musical conviction.

In 1964, Hitomi Kasuya was the youngest girl on a similar tour. Last night 9-year-old Hitomi played Vitali's "Chaconne" with a firm understanding of its challenges.

But the "showman" of the evening was Akihiro Miura, who performed the Presto movement from Vivaldi's A-minor Concerto with polish. Intonation wavered now and then—but after all he's only 6!

The performances brought tears to the eyes of many string teachers in the audience. And at least one critic bawled a little over the present string shortage in our country, brought into such stark relief by these Japanese child-musicians.

Chapter IX

*Home-Made Suzuki**

The success or failure of the Suzuki method of teaching the violin to young children depends on the parents and the environment they create in the home. From playing good recordings for the baby to encouraging the teen-age artist, the parents' role is crucial. As a former Cleveland Orchestra man (now connected with schools) puts it, "Perhaps we should import some parents from Japan!"

The parent who takes the three-year-old child to a short lesson once a week is the teacher in the home the other six days of the week. Where nothing happens in the home (or where what happens is at cross-purposes with the violin teacher's instructions), the prospect is hopeless. Fortunately, there *are* parents who can find some time to devote to their children and who show interest in them. Sometimes both parents come to lessons.

Often a parent says, "I am no musician. How can I teach my child?" The answer is this: By playing the record or tape being studied, regularly, for the child at home; by following the teacher's instructions, regularly, at home; and finally, by patient encouragement of the child, regularly, at home. There is no place in this system for nagging one's child because some other child is one piece ahead. Worst of all is the parent who is a professional musician and who pushes his child unmercifully, giving all sorts of instructions

_____
*Reprinted by permission from *String Along*, Ohio String Teachers Association Bulletin, April 5, 1969.

counter to the teacher's suggestions. The poor child ends up completely confused!

One case I remember well. (This mother was a real case-worker.) One week she showed me an elaborate nameplate she had attached to her child's violin case. Another week she had knitted a beautiful cover for the case. She devoted a lot of time to these projects but never got around to doing anything about what was inside the case. Fringe benefits, no doubt!

Family groups bound together by a common interest in music-making have always interested me. Many such groups have played in the seven College-Community String Festivals I have led here. The record number from one family was seven—father and mother and five children. The only reason the sixth of the children did not play was that she was away at college at the time. They all sang at home and played several instruments. What a family, what a home!

Last December I presented a program called "Home-Made Suzuki" for the Oberlin Woman's Club. At first four children (ages four to eleven) played solos, each accompanied by a parent. One of these parents had recently won the first international competition for electronic compositions, but on this program he was piano accompanist for his seven-year-old daughter in a Lully "Gavotte."

Next, two pairs of children from two families played violin duets with piano accompaniment. Then we had two different family quartets play, each with a young son playing cello.

After a few musical games played by all the children together, we closed our program with three Christmas Carols, played by five members of one family. The father of this group (who has quite a sense of humor) called them the "Crap Family" but to my ears and eyes this was the nicest Christmas music of the season!

Chapter X

Talent Education Tour, Summer, 1969

The twentieth Summer School of the Talent Education Institute was held in Matsumoto, Japan, from July 29 through August 2. Around 460 children, many teachers and teacher-trainees, and several hundred parents attended. Our group included fifteen teachers from the States. This summer session is one of the three national meetings held each year, and is the only one where so many children can be observed studying everything from the beginning "Variations" to advanced concertos.

It is a bee-hive of activity, involving the Talent Education Kaikan (building), the large City Auditorium next door, and the Shonan High School a few blocks away. Between the opening ceremony on Wednesday morning and the closing ceremony Saturday afternoon, selected pieces from the ten volumes of the Suzuki Violin Method were given concentrated study and cello repertoire was worked on. Classrooms were labeled according to the composition being studied; a sign, "Handel Sonata No. 4," on the door meant a roomful of children, parents, and several teachers engrossed in studying this work. About twenty selections were studied in great detail in this way during the summer school.

Large group lessons on a varied repertoire were given by Dr. Suzuki daily. It is always a pleasure to watch him work with children, as he sharpens their reactions and makes them laugh and have a great time, without realizing that they are being taught and taught very well. During a break he lights a cigarette in his "pipe" (as he calls his cigarette-holder), takes a Japanese sign off the wall and brings it back to us to translate. The translation is "No Smoking."

During one of these large group sessions, the following idea occurred to me. From the big group of children playing on the stage, one could close his eyes and pick any ten—they could tour the United States successfully!

Once during a "private" lesson on stage Suzuki lay on his back on the floor to study the bowing, violin hold, etc. from below, as an auto mechanic would examine a car from underneath it. Another time while a girl was playing he parted her black hair and produced the proof of his statement, "She has an ear!"

Playing the dictation game with a group (they were to play back whatever he played) he got them so keyed up they would join him before he had finished playing the first note. I can still see the expression on the face of one chubby little five-year-old with two pigtails as she watched him like a hawk, waiting to pounce on whatever he played. (Izumi Terada, the youngest child on the 1969 Tour of the States.) This ability to make children laugh and relax, while sharpening them to split-second reactions, is the mark of a great teacher.

Evenings were given over to concerts, very enjoyable despite the heat and child-noise in the City Auditorium. Several good cello soloists were included and some child pianists were heard. The young pianists could not reach an octave, of course, and they used a special arm-finger technique at this age, but their playing was solid, confident, and very musical, just like that of the tiny violinists. They required a special chair-adjustment and used a footstool. The little pianists elicited many ohs and ahs from the American visitors.

The first evening concert began with the Lalo Cello

Concerto in D minor, followed by Bach's Solo Violin Sonata in G minor. Then a Talent Education alumna, Hiroko Yamada, played the Mozart Concerto No. 5 in A like the seasoned artist she is. Now a first violinist in the Rotterdam Symphony, formerly in the first violin section of the Berlin Radio Symphony, she was in Matsumoto visiting her mother during a vacation of several weeks.

The concert closed with a group of selections by Handel, Mennini, Van Vactor, Holst, and Strauss played by the Teacher Trainees String Orchestra, conducted by William Starr of the University of Tennessee, who had spent the past year in Matsumoto. The violins had a magnificent sound, but the bottom parts were less impressive in this group. Violin solos were well played by Concertmistress Hiroko Toba who, with Miss Yamada, had taught for me in Oberlin. (Miss Toba had become *Mrs.* Toba, as she had married and her husband had taken her name.)

The following evening's concert began with Bach piano pieces played by two children, followed by the Mozart Sonata in B-Flat for violin and piano. Yuko Honda, who had taught in Seattle, Oberlin, and Eastman, played well three movements of Bach's E major Partita. A Tokyo cellist played the Boellman "Symphonic Variations." Ending this concert was a fine performance of the Bach A minor Concerto for violin and string orchestra. The soloist was Eiko Suzuki, a young artist who had taught three years for me and now seems like a daughter to Mrs. Cook and myself.

Friday night's concert began with Beethoven and Mozart piano sonatas, followed by a Starr Family Concert which I dubbed "Twinkle, Twinkle, Little Starrs." Judith played Corelli's "La Folia," Timmy a part of Eccles' G minor Sonata, Kathleen the first movement of the Haydn Cello Concerto in D, Michael, Judith, Timmy and Mr. Starr Suzuki's "Perpetual Motion," and finally Mr. Starr played Bruch's

"Adagio" and his own version of Suzuki's "Twinkle Variations," complete with glissandi, left-hand pizzicati, etc. This
brought down the house. Mrs. Starr played piano for all the
family selections. This entire family had spent an interesting
and profitable year in Matsumoto. A group of selections by
a very good chamber orchestra, the Concertino di Kyoto,
closed the program.

There were many additional features scattered throughout the summer school such as a chamber music program
of string quartet movements played by teacher trainees and
concerts by large groups. One person could not begin to
take in all the activities going on simultaneously.

After the close of summer school, Mr. Suzuki gave a
series of individual lessons to children from different teachers. Many concertos and sonatas were studied. Suzuki made
his suggestions clear to the children, parents, and teachers
involved. He is very frank with his teachers, but in such a
way that they do not take offense. (I once heard him tell a
teacher, after a long class recital, that *one* student had good
form!)

Coda

At the start of one large-group session, Suzuki had the
children yell out to their parents (repeating after him):
"We are good boys and girls, so please educate us. When
we practice at home every day, it makes trouble. Sorry
about that!" This rather common practice of having the
children repeat in unison what the teacher says reminds me
of the demonstrating university students we saw in Tokyo,
marching with banners and repeating phrases after the loud-
speaker on a truck. The Japanese seem to have a predilec-
tion for group chanting in unison, repeating what someone
tells them. This becomes almost a form of hypnotism for the
marching students.

President Masaru Ibuka of Sony Corporation told us in Tokyo of his interest in Talent Education. (Sony has its own schools for workers' children, near some of its factories.) He said he has given up on university students and is concentrating on the education of *young children* now, hoping for better things in the future!

Suzuki sounded a bit pessimistic when he said the twentieth century is apparently to be given over to technology. But he hopes that the twenty-first century will show a greater interest in people and their development.

There were some lighter touches to our tour. One lady asked if the Japan Alps were the same as the Austrian; a sign on one of our Tokyo buses read "American Spring Teachers Tour"; some people in our party began to mix their l's and r's: "I'm leady for runch"; a girlie book was advertised "For Men With Yen."

At the summer school, one little boy went to sleep after lunch and fell off his chair—*on his head!* (Fortunately, his violin and bow were not damaged.) We heard of a young violinist with a small tape recorder strapped on his back, playing an endless tape constantly. Would you believe, he made remarkable progress in one week!

Mr. Starr reported (confirming my own observation) that he had never seen a mothers' class studying violin in Japan, despite reports that the mothers always start first. (Most mothers' violin sound and musical "form" are *not* good for a model, and the visual effect of a mother playing on a tiny violin may be described as "Funny Girl!") He also told us that there is no future tense in the Japanese language, possibly explaining why it is hard to pin down a Japanese to a definite promise for the future. "Perhaps," "maybe," or "God willing," not "I will do it."

At a session with Tokyo teachers we learned that the six symphony orchestras in Tokyo give no children's concerts.

There is no connection between these orchestras and Talent Education, but about one-fifth of the symphony string players come from Talent Education. Tokyo lessons for the children now average about 2,500 yen per month ($6.95) for one lesson a week. Beginners pay less, advanced students more. About 5,000 children are now studying by the Suzuki method in Japan.

Violinist Sheldon Rotenberg of the Boston Symphony, who had just finished his exchange year with the Japan Philarmonic, said that symphony players in Tokyo get a salary of about $150 per month and end up with about $22 a week. The American exchange players are enthusiastic about their experiences in Japan, however. (The young Suzuki teachers in the States who make $400 per month, plus living and travel, are doing all right!)

I close this all-too-brief report of the tour by repeating something I have said many times before: *Children are important in Japan!*

Chapter XI

*Shinichi Suzuki**

My first meeting with Mr. Suzuki in person was at Hane-da Airport, Tokyo, in March of 1963. When Mrs. Cook and I arrived at 2:00 A.M., we were met by Mr. and Mrs. Suzuki, Dr. Masaaki Honda, and two of his daughters. On the long taxi trip to our hotel in Tokyo, Mr. Suzuki held one of our heavy bags on his lap. By three o'clock of that March morning we had decided that these were unusual people and that Mr. Suzuki was a remarkable man. The years since then have amply corroborated the correctness of our first impression.

I can see him in my mind, sitting on a davenport in our daughter's home, pulling on one end of an old blanket, while two of our grandchildren were pulling (and laughing) on the other end. This was in the evening of a long workshop day, but he was not too tired to play with the children. Again, I can see him on a plane from Philadelphia to Cleveland, holding the sack for a young Japanese violinist who became sick every time she flew. He was her constant and comforting companion on all their many flights.

Near the Cleveland Art Museum a warning road sign had been knocked over into the street where it was a menace to the cars whizzing by. Many drivers cursed as they dodged

---

*Mr. Suzuki's excellent book, *Nurtured by Love*, (Exposition Press, Jericho, N. Y., 1969), explains his philosophy and gives many details of his life. I shall try in this chapter to avoid duplicating material contained in his book.

it, or looked back with disgust, but none did anything about it. Mr. Suzuki ducked out into the street, got the sign and put it upright where it belonged.

Mrs. Suzuki told me that once as they were driving in Matsumoto they came to a crowd gathered around a fierce fight between two huge dogs. The dogs' masters and many spectators were standing around, helpless. Mr. Suzuki jumped out of the car, grabbed one of the dogs by its tail, and hung on until the fight was stopped. "We must do something" he says, "It's not enough just to know." (To him, the violin means *knowing* and *doing!*)

To understand his teaching, one must first understand him as a man. "Art is heart" he says. In teaching as in living, *he puts the heart before the course.* I can still see him playing for Reber Johnson in a rest home, then asking Reber what he should do to improve his playing.

Very modest and humble, he gives a picture off his wall or anything else he can find to his guest as a gift. Mrs. Suzuki had me trick him into a tailor's shop in Tokyo to get a new suit. He had persistently refused to spend the money on anything for himself! His money goes into Talent Education.

Sir Thomas Beecham once told me, "Nothing worthwhile ever pays for itself." (At Oberlin I always tried to keep the cost of our Suzuki lessons as low as possible, not to exclude those who couldn't afford to pay more.) Talent Education in Japan has constant financial problems, too. Often it has seemed that money is the *main* consideration! Suzuki says many people think he is better at spending than at making it, but he has done all right in both ways.

"I do what I can" he says. Performing in Suwa, he made a mistake, stopped and said "Is not right," then played the passage again, correctly. "Publicum liked." He told an advanced student "If you don't play better than I after a year, I'll drop you!" "Higher, higher" he urges persistently. "We must do better than the record." (But with the wealth of recordings available now, the finest artists in the world can play and teach every day *anywhere*.) Again and again, I have found that a person *feels* better and *does* better after being with Suzuki.

Eiko and Kako, young Japanese violin teachers, sat on the front steps of our home, looking eagerly down the street. They had not seen Mr. Suzuki for a year or two, and now he was due from the airport to conduct a workshop for us. When he did not arrive on time, they went a block down the street and stood watching like a couple of young children. Working their way block by block, they were downtown when he finally arrived. Dinner was ready when they came happily home with him.

As soon as dinner was over, the two girls went upstairs to get their violins. Not a word was said. We gathered in the living room and Suzuki went to work on the girls, individually and together, in a long and joyful "reunion lesson." I have witnessed these delightful affairs many times, but I never cease to marvel at a teacher who maintains such a relationship with his former students!

Although their teaching methods are different, Shinichi Suzuki and Ivan Galamian are similar in their fanaticism for teaching violin and improving every student they contact. Both can work long hours, seven days a week. Neither has a child of his own, but how many "children" they have in all the students they have taught! Both are soft-spoken and mild-mannered, but each can really "lay it on the line" when indignant. Each can diagnose instantly any violinistic weakness and prescribe what to do for it. Both men are at the age where they feel they have no time to *waste*. It has been a privilege to know such dedicated teachers.

Suzuki says "I never tire of teaching children." His wife says "He has a way with children." Dr. Honda says "Suzuki doesn't tire, his spirit is strong." Dr. Suzuki believes he has a certain power of healing in his hands, and his "treatment" consists of vibrating his hand near an injury. When Yuko Honda caught her finger in the car door, he shook his hand in the air, near the injured finger, for some time. This power, he says, was passed on to him as a young man from a hermit in the mountains. His study was completed by a midnight test of passing a red-hot piece of iron through his hands without being burned. There is no question about his still having power in his hands with violin and bow. When asked about his age, he says he is too busy to "go anywhere." The Japanese consistently refuse to discuss what will happen to Talent Education when Mr. Suzuki *must* "go somewhere." They say "We don't think of that." (It's the Zen emphasis on the *here and now*, not the future. Not a bad way to live?)

His patience in insisting on repetition until a thing is completely learned is well-known. He often tells a student to practice a spot 10,000 times, or explains a long bow as "10,000 points." Practice the same piece over and over, "not English, French, Italian, German, and Japanese on successive days." Music and violin playing must become part of oneself, like speaking. There are no "dropouts" from using one's mother tongue. We Americans don't have to think "Now I am going to speak English." But he laughs when I tell him *his* English is "made in Japan."

A teacher at a workshop asked Suzuki about giving the Seashore tests to decide who shall study music. Reply: "Shall we give English test to babies, then say, this one shall learn to speak English, this one shall not (send to Italy)?"

"Who ever learned to speak with his eyes?" The most common question asked about his students is "Yes, but can they *read?*" He replies with another question "Yes. Can *you* play without music?" When a student at a workshop had finished playing a movement from a Handel Sonata, laboriously reading every note from the music, he said "You read notes very well!" (This remark was misinterpreted as a compliment.) Over and over he returns to the way we learn to speak: "We don't learn to speak by *etuden*."

Matsumoto mathematics: He tells a child to play a spot ten times while Suzuki counts. The counting goes "11111 222222 3333333," etc. "Tempo di Matsumoto" is on the crisp side—"Educate to tempo, the teacher must not go to the child's tempo." "Piano is a little tone-deaf"—there is no piano in the studio in Matsumoto where he does most of his teaching.

He loves to analyze. When we became very hungry, while driving at night on an Interstate highway, he declared that his wife laughed too much, Mrs. Cook and I didn't speak, and he could smell the Howard Johnson neon sign! He says he would invite Mozart, Schumann and a few other composers to the Japanese tea ceremony, but *not* Beethoven (*he* wouldn't fit in). Of the Kabuki-Za theater in Tokyo, he says he doesn't know what is going on there! "Often concours are more for *teachers* than for students." As an examination for his teacher-trainees, the one who, without request, brings him his ashtray is "ready to teach." Looking at Niagara Falls, hearing the roar of the falls and then seeing the quiet river far below: "Forte and piano." "You can't force the growth of a plant by pulling on its leaves—good growing conditions are needed. So in education!"

He is fond of "Instant Suzuki"—of improvising on the spot. A little glue on the soundpost or bassbar of a violin may produce "instant silvertone." Instant programming, organizing a chorus, and sumie painting are some of his extemporaneous delights. William Starr says Suzuki may change his mind fifty times in a month. He *can* be very mercurial and pixie-like, anything but static.

On the other hand, he can be very methodical and per-

sistent. He says it took him ten years to perfect Volume I
of his Violin Method. The "Japanese Carpenter's Song" and
"Nagoya Lullaby" have been his violin solo "program" for
years. When he played Japanese melodies for Szigeti and
the other judges of the 1969 Montreal Concours, then asked
for suggestions about his playing, all he got was "Very
good," "I enjoyed it," etc.) He listened to Kreisler's recording of the slow movement of the Grieg C minor Sonata for
forty hours, to analyze what Kreisler did to produce the
sound Suzuki admires so much. No one could estimate the
number of pre-daylight hours he has spent in making by
hand the diplomas he gives to each of his young "graduates."

One of my friends, after observing him in a two-week
workshop, said Suzuki could "sell gold bricks to almost
anyone." But Suzuki himself says he is a prophet without
honor in his own country. The Director of a large music
school in Tokyo said *nothing* when I expressed admiration
for Suzuki and his children. Opposition by traditionally
trained musicians to Suzuki and his ideas is well-known, and
it exists for a number of reasons. A very competent psychologist told me "It takes someone out of the rut to come up
with something out of the rut." On seeing the wonders of
our new Conservatory building for the first time he asked
"Do the students work better?"

He does not regard singing as the best first approach to
instrumental study, but emphasizes rhythm, dance, and
the staccato principle. Thus, the first thing a child plays on
the violin is a quick rhythmic figure involving stopping the
bow, not a long legato line. "*Allegro* does not come from
singing," he says.

Individual lessons come first, then group playing. With
a group, work only on what the children can already *play*,
not new material. "Children like what they can do."

Concentrate on *one thing only* at a lesson. He cannot

give a "thirty-minute lesson"; his lesson lasts until the student understands. He can always show what he wants, and he plays on the student's violin—"Violin is *ok*." Tonalization (vocalization on the violin, developing tone) is a part of every lesson. He teaches *music* and *tone,* not scales, and says he doesn't know how a G-Flat scale should be played— is it crescendo or diminuendo? He told one teacher that she had a one-hundred-dollar bow and a five-dollar tone.

He uses the *plateau* method in his pieces. For example, the first six pieces in Volume 1 make up a plateau—they are all on the same technical level. But each new piece introduces some little new feature. "Papillon" contains thirds, involving skipping a finger. (The first piece, "Variations," has used only scale-wise fingering.) "Warnung" uses downbow phrasing, requiring lifting and setting the bow to start each new section down-bow. It also introduces a fingered fifth across two strings, played at first by lifting the finger and setting it on the new string. "Lied" is more legato in style than the preceding pieces and is played with smoother, longer bowing. It is good for making dynamic contrast, also. "Die Kinder" introduces up-bow phrasing, used all the way through the piece. "Mailied" introduces the dotted quarter-eighth rhythm and the tonic chord in an octave range. Add to these technical features the subtle differences in mood and style of these first six pieces and a very cleverly arranged plateau is realized. Such things do not just "happen."

"Add, don't finish" he says. Use easy material to improve ability. If the teacher *demands, something happens!*

One notes often the great value of his sense of humor, and sees that those of his teachers who share it do better than those who do not. When a student plays an out-of-tune pitch, he calls it a "home-made C." When four of his students play the Tchaikovsky Concerto differently, although all are listening to the same Oistrakh recording, he says "must be something wrong with their ears!" He laughs when he tells of the first radio broadcast given in Japan by the Suzuki String Quartet (four brothers). The violist was the most emotional one; in climaxes he would rise up off his chair. When he did this during the broadcast the announcer thought he wanted his chair removed, and obliged. When violist Suzuki went to sit down again he ended up on the floor, and the broadcast came to an abrupt halt. The announcer's explanation over the air: "Machine kaput." Violinist Suzuki delights in showing how slowly a Japanese quartet he once heard played the opening three chords of the Finale of Haydn's *Emperor Quartet*: Chord—(take smoke)—chord —(take another smoke)—chord. I suppose this tempo might be called *Adagio con tobacco!* (When Mr. Suzuki is happy he usually begins to hum—as he did when we would go out for a ride in the evening.)

He has written "I just want to make good citizens. If a child hears good music from the day of his birth, and learns to play it himself, he develops sensitivity, discipline, and endurance. He gets a beautiful heart. By developing their musical sense and helping each other our children will bring a better world for tomorrow."

It may be noted here that, despite the rather common impression that Talent Education in Japan is a one-man operation, there are many other good teachers in the movement. But there is no question about who is in charge. Mildmannered though he usually is, he can assume a dictatorial role at times. And there is a certain "Messianic" tendency, too. The kind of power Suzuki wields in his "kingdom" in Japan would be impossible for one person in the United States—there is too much independence and diversity here!

After Mr. Suzuki's first visit to our campus, the wife of an English professor described her impression of him: "His talk is *non-intellectual*." She meant this as a compliment, although in some collegiate circles the intellect is worshiped as supreme. I think I would call him "super-intellectual," according to my belief that the highest experiences in life are *above* the level of the intellect.

He is not much interested in the musicological approach. The last piece in Volume III is called "Loure." Actually, it is a "Bourrée" from one of the cello suites of J. S. Bach. The source of many pieces is not given, as for instance, the Handel Bourrée in Volume II, which comes from a flute sonata. Little points, to be sure, but some musicians *do* bring them up and ask questions.

A child is often asked to say an important point ten times before playing, such as "My intonation is not so good. My first finger is too high." The ear must not be trained by the fingers (or by the teacher's tongue). The ear is properly trained by good models—by hearing repeatedly musical, in-tune performances of fine music. The best models available are chosen for listening. To the common criticism of using a recording as a first learning model, I have often said that it takes a lot of crust for a teacher to imply that "I am a better violinist than Stern, Heifetz, Oistrakh or ———."

To a child who is swaying excessively he says "Pianists don't move the piano around the stage while playing." "Open string second finger" means to try to match the resonance of the second finger's tone to the full sound heard from the open string. The teacher's position for observing a lesson is "where the student's violin points." To American students he often says "Don't *think so hard*, just play!" When a child gets a piece to the stage where most teachers consider it learned and ready to drop, Suzuki says "Then my lessons on it begin." Emphasizing the importance of an early start in music, I once had him give a short "lesson" to two unborn babies! (Only time will tell how this works out.)

Playing with eyes closed or in a darkened room is excellent for developing tone. In fact, a dark room is best for developing photographs, tone, or love! The bow stick exists only for the hair. A relaxed hold of the bow is like a *young* man, not a stiff and slow *old* man. To a student Suzuki sometimes may say "You carry an elephant with your bow. Now carry a mouse." Hold the bow by the screw, by the hair, or by the tip (reversed) some for practice. Hold at different places in the bow. Hold the bow like a club sometimes, to get a solid sound. Practically all very young children are taught at first to hold the thumb *beneath* the frog, on the silver ring. "All is round"—the sun, the moon, the earth, the shape of the two hands in playing.

A favorite Suzuki bowing exercise consists of playing all sorts of things with only the thumb and middle finger holding the bow. This goes directly back to *Joseph Joachim.* Suzuki's teacher in Berlin, Karl Klingler, was a Joachim graduate.

"Touch" means to set the bow on the string, then play. Without preparation, the *slip* tone results. With stiff fingers and arm, the *press* tone results. Don't bow with *hand* only, any more than you walk with feet only. Arm=leg. Whole arm plays bow. Play elbow, feel hand. Elbow, hand and tip of bow all go together. "Arm tone," not "finger tone." We can't move a piano with our fingers only; we have to put our whole body into it. Keep arm weight on when changing string, too. *Hand* leads on change to string of lower pitch, *elbow* on change to string of higher pitch. Use a *strong* hold of the bow for pp, *soft* hold for ff. Work to get a strong sound at the tip of the bow. The tip is very important—learn to control it in bow-gymnastics, and think of it often while playing. In performance there should not be always home runs—sometimes a *bunt!* Down and up bow are *one* motion. For a long note at end of phrase, use a slow bow.

When a child is "sawing" with the bow in a circular motion, Suzuki stands so the bow hits him in the stomach at the end of its circle, and then he says, "Ouch!" Then the youngster draws the bow correctly and misses him. Suzuki sometimes balances his bow on its tip in his hand, flips it through a circle in the air, and then catches it at the frog. "Casals doesn't do this," Suzuki says, "but I am an *educator*." Amen! *And what an educator!*

Chapter XII

Five Graduates of Talent Education

Hiroko I

Hiroko Yamada was born in Manchuria and came to Japan after World War II. She started violin at the age of six in the first group of children in Talent Education with Mr. Suzuki. After graduating from high school she taught Talent Education before coming to America.

Miss Yamada taught and studied for two years at Oberlin, studied and played for two summers at Aspen, and played for one summer at Dartmouth. Her home was in Matsumoto, and she had the Zen concept of time that Mrs. Suzuki calls "Matsumoto time"—more free than in the West. To her, a lesson presents an idea, not a time-unit. Her own lessons with Mr. Suzuki had a wide range of duration. "If twenty minutes, fine—if it takes two hours, ok."

She said training the mothers was the hardest thing in the States. She emphasized the importance of "firm-mind" or "force" (stick-to-it-iveness), and felt that many of our children and parents tend to give up before they get started. (Her first impression of Oberlin College students was that they were a grim bunch, rushing about with their heads down.) Many teachers work too hard, and don't leave enough to the child. Make the child think and do more; don't spoil him by doing everything for him! Self-control is very important.

Concentration training is the first step for the very young beginner. It may be for only one minute at first, but attention *must* be paid. This is Mr. Suzuki's idea when he says a beginning child's lesson lasts "until the child yawns."

Don't press bow, was Hiroko's frequent admonition. In working to jack up the tempo, she often said the children play fast in Japan. (I have noticed that a Japanese child frequently tends to go faster in a hard spot, instead of slacking off in such a place.) Hiroko told the children of a professional violinist "If you want my lesson, you do *my* homework."

She missed some lessons, but so did her own teacher. The Japanese teachers in the States tend to mirror what they observe, and respond as they are treated. They become Westernized quickly. Orchestra conductors complained of cuts and no practice (laziness) on the part of the Matsumoto girls. They were often very weak and sickly, except when they really *wanted* to do something—then they were strong as bulls! Piano study did not seem to work out for them.

Hiroko said "I don't want to play violin. My mother and Mr. Suzuki want." But she could play, and with a beautiful Saino-Kyoiku tone. She gave public performances of the Mozart-Kreisler "Rondo," the Saint-Saens "Rondo Capriccioso," the Chausson "Poème," the Ravel "Tzigane," the Brahms Sonata in D minor and Quartet in A minor (as first violinist). When playing the Brahms "Sonata" with music, she found it confusing to "see bowings and fingerings I am not playing." She much preferred playing without the music.

In preparing for a performance, she would use records and tapes for all they were worth. She got her money's worth out of everything—no waste! After winning over Juilliard and Oberlin concertmasters in an Aspen competition to solo with orchestra, she played the Chausson "Poème." For the performance she was loaned an Italian violin to use instead of her own Japanese instrument. Since she did not have her tape-recorder or tapes with her at Aspen, she could not prepare in her usual way; I am sure she could have given a better final performance if prepared in her own way. Despite all her self-control in public performance, she was beside herself with excitement when Mr. Suzuki and the Japanese children came to the States for the first tour in 1964.

Beneath the Japanese smiles and pleasantness there can also be hardness and aggressiveness. Dr. Honda once told me that the Japanese are a shy people, but once they overcome their shyness, they tend to go too far the other way. Saving face is really important to Orientals. Hiroko was still something of a "child-violinist" herself, at twenty-three! It was difficult for her to work with anyone else, and she had a furious temper. She said that the Talent Education teachers in Japan expressed high ideals to the children, but fought tooth and nail among themselves. She wanted to get away from that. (Unfortunately, music teachers fight among themselves *anywhere*.)

From Oberlin, she went to Berlin, where she played in the Radio Symphony Orchestra. (A postcard report said their concerts were always "clouded.")

Hiroko II

The second teacher proposed by Mr. Suzuki was vetoed by Miss Yamada, who said "I leave if she comes." The second teacher who *did* come was Hiroko Toba, also from Matsumoto, where she had studied and taught. She was in Oberlin one year, and played at Dartmouth the following summer.

She was given the beginners to teach and definitely played second fiddle to the older Hiroko throughout the year. Her English was not advanced enough for her to take courses. She studied violin, played in orchestra and a string quartet. She gave no solo performances while here, in spite of my urging. She could play, but I think she felt inferior to her older colleague and did not want to play for that reason. (Or perhaps she was deliberately kept down.)

She taught the little children while on her knees, in the approved Japanese fashion. She had lots of patience with the little ones and was a good teacher for them. She, too, missed some lessons and did the great Oriental disappearing act when parents or I tried to find her. She signed a contract for a second year, but did not return. She is now married and living in Matsumoto.

Yuko

Miss Yuko Honda is the daughter of Dr. Masaaki Honda, a pediatrician in Fujisawa and a Director of Talent Education in Japan for many years. Dr. Honda has accompanied all of the Talent Education tours of the States. Yuko had studied by both Talent Education and other methods in Japan. She met us in Tokyo, and we heard her play in her home and in Mr. Suzuki's home. She assisted Mr. Suzuki in his three-week workshop in Oberlin during the summer of 1965.

Yuko was a fine young woman, spoke English well, and was pleasant to work with. She taught a class of teachers at Western Reserve University in Cleveland in the afternoons. She was very busy, but did not complain.

She played well, but was not one of the most outstanding violinists in Talent Education. She played "La Folia," the Eccles "Sonata," and Kreisler's "La Gitana" for us. She got some of the "Saino-Kyoiku tone" from Mr. Suzuki, and served as guinea pig in some of his tests, such as doing math problems while playing a Vivaldi concerto. She was emotional and cried easily—when she did this the first time she played for us in her home, I thought perhaps she was being forced. She appeared in some films during her period of study and teaching in Seattle.

Yuko later taught a year at Eastman. She was married, soon after playing at the 1969 Matsumoto Summer School, to a Japanese conducting student, Mr. Nobuo Takahashi, and they planned to be at Drake University, Des Moines, Iowa for the 1969-70 school year. I last saw Yuko with the touring Japanese children in October of 1969.

Eiko

Eiko Suzuki (no relative) is an outstanding example of training by the Talent Education method. She began her study at two and a half and her teacher was Mr. Kondo (former concertmaster of NHK Orchestra) except for some lessons with Mr. Suzuki during the three years before she came to Oberlin. Her home was in Toyohashi. Her father worked for Talent Education, not as a teacher, but in promotion and business phases. He wrote a book about Eiko's education—in Japanese, of course.

When she was small, her parents put her on a table to practice and danced to her playing, or her father conducted while she played—anything to get her to practice. At four she knew by memory one hundred haiku (the Japanese poems used by Talent Education for the memory training of young children). I have a tape of her playing the Mozart D major Concerto when she was eight, and one of the Saint-Saens Concerti when she was thirteen.

When we were in Japan in 1963 her father served as our guide much of the time. He was nicknamed "Kamikaze" because of his quick motions and ability to do many things at once. During our trip we heard Eiko play many times— Tchaikovsky "Concerto," Mozart-Kreisler "Rondo," Bach "Chaconne," etc. We were, of course, much impressed with her. When she came to Oberlin in 1965, she already had a huge repertoire. She was with us for three years and two summers.

During that three-year period she played every time I asked her, without question or hesitation. She gave innumerable performances: Concerti by Mozart, Tchaikovsky, Sibelius, Brahms (with orchestra, after winning a competition), recitals, and many solos. I took her to the first Suzuki Institute held in the summer of 1966 at the Eastman School, where she played the Tchaikovsky three times, after not having touched it for over a year. (Mr. Suzuki said it had been in the "freezer.") I often thought that her playing worked on the transistor principle—it came on right away—not like a tube that must warm up before it gives a picture. Her attitude toward performance is shown by this quote from a letter from Japan: "My recital on June 21st went ok. Many people came for it, I was so glad. I played without mistake. Well, every time, I never felt to be satisfied with my play, but feel always have to try to be better for them."

On summer evenings, after the dinner dishes were done, Eiko would go to her room, get out her violin and play through all the pieces in one of the volumes of the Suzuki Violin Method. (She knew all of them well enough to play in her sleep.) Then she would finish by playing a major concerto. The program changed every night. Meanwhile, I would be lying in the porch hammock enjoying the concert—a very pleasant Midsummer Night's Dream!

As previously noted, the first question every American teacher asks is "Can they read?" Of course Eiko faced this when she first came to the States. She was assigned a Beethoven Sonata which she had not studied or heard. After three lessons she performed the complete work in public. She respectfully used a stand with music on it, but since I had heard her play the entire piece from memory, I knew how much she was using the music. The burning question was answered.

After her initial rehearsal as first violin in a string quartet she came to our home in tears and said she couldn't play string quartet. I doubted this, and found the problem to be her English. She couldn't understand what her colleagues said at first, nor could she express her own ideas to them. Her quartet later performed the Schoenberg "Second Quartet," and she was concertmistress of the Oberlin Orchestra in such works as the Schoenberg "Variations." When Eiko left, nobody was asking if she could read.

She was absolutely reliable; if I told her someone was coming for a lesson on Thursday at three o'clock I had no need to give it another thought. She was a good practical psychologist, too. One of her boy friends always asked her "Why?" in regard to all the points she made about playing the violin. Her reply was *"Do* it first, then figure out *why!"* (His problem was that he couldn't do it.)

We once took our Talent Education children to Columbus to play two programs for a convention of music teachers. Kazuko, Eiko's assistant, was to play the Mendelssohn "Concerto" on the first program, and Eiko the Sibelius on the second. The night before we were to go, Kako's teacher called and said she couldn't play, she had broken down and cried at her last lesson. When I told Eiko, she said "She *thinks* too much! *You can't think like that."* So Eiko went to see Kako.

The next day we went to Columbus. Nothing was said, so I didn't know if Kako would play or not. When the time came for the Mendelssohn on the program, Kako played it— and well. I still don't know what Eiko said or did, but whatever it was, it worked! Kako was not the only person who gained strength from Eiko.

Eiko speeded up my granddaughter and had her small

fingers fairly flying on the Bach "Musette," which Jenny wanted to play for everyone. Another of Eiko's young students played his current piece three times for company, and wanted to play it more. *Good teaching.* When my wife and I returned from a Scandinavian trip, Eiko was waiting for us, dressed in a beautiful kimono and obi. *Good personal relations.*

On a mock student recital program, the Fiocco "Allegro" and Gossec "Gavotte" were played by Eiko Numanami, violin. Eiko Suzuki bowed, and Kazuko Numanami fingered (Mr. Suzuki says "Each plays only 50%.") The second piece they played while fluttering Japanese fans in their free hands. This brought them a standing ovation.

Much more might be written about Eiko, but this is perhaps enough to show why our hearts were so sad when she left to see her father shortly before he died of cancer. She said she didn't feel as though she were leaving—"It seemed to be happening to somebody else." She said the same thing once after she had played, expressing the same kind of dream-like detachment. Eiko's touching "goodbye note" is treasured by Mrs. Cook and myself. The letters she wrote after the death of her father touch the heart and reveal a noble spirit. (Word has just come from Eiko that she has married a Japanese cellist, Masayoshi Kataoka, and they will be living in St. Louis.)

Kako

Kazuko Numanami is the daughter of a fishmonger in Matsumoto. In addition to her study of Talent Education she had studied for a year at Toho Music School in Tokyo. (She didn't like it there.) She came to us to assist Eiko, and later taught on her own.

Whereas Eiko could get along with any teacher and

adopt what she liked from him, Kako couldn't really get along with any other violin teacher except Mr. Suzuki. When anything in her playing was criticized, she felt that Mr. Suzuki was being criticized, and she promptly "got her back up." In fact, when she went back to Japan she resented even Mr. Suzuki's criticism! Her tendency to cry easily caused Suzuki to say "Kazuko should take up boxing, not crying."

She played some chamber music and orchestra while here, but did very little solo playing. Like Miss Toba, she was overshadowed in that field. Her Mendelssohn has been mentioned before. She bowed to the audience in a very reverent way before playing a Japanese piece, "Haru no umi" (Spring Sea.) She played some unaccompanied Bach at a workshop session.

Kako was a good teacher, especially with little children. She analyzed carefully and stressed good form and the importance of fundamentals. She had a retarded child shut her eyes and count to ten. Teaching this child to put away her violin in its case was a major accomplishment. She had a restless child stand straight (at "attention") while she counted. This was called "planting." A plant can't grow if it moves about all the time; it must stay in the same place to take root! Here we have the first stage in the discipline of a child.

She said a teacher must be alive and fast to keep the children alert. She had children clap, jump or hop *after* her, then *with* her; constant change jacks them up. She often asked "Are you hungry?" (Slow and weak). She had children yell, "let go," then they were ready to play violin without inhibitions. She believed in keeping a small child on the Twinkle Variations for a year, to develop good form. This practice encountered the usual resistance from parents. She complained that the Conservatory faculty did not understand Talent Education.

Self-respect first, she insisted. Children learn most from each other. She called the fingers of the left hand "mountains"—"mountains are high." She taught *curved* fingers on both hands, and said straight, stiff fingers were the most common fault with American children. The thumb should lean *against* the frog, not the stick. The first and third fingers have the important function of making tone. When a stiff pinky presses on the stick, the tone is weak. "Bow like putting Scotch tape on paper." After she had heard of Casals' use of the rainbow form in shaping a phrase, the word "rainbow" was much used in her teaching. "Hold three eggs while playing"—one in the palm of each hand, one in the left arm-pit. "Don't break!"

She and her boy friend pretended to be "Cybel and David," age five and seven. She was mixed-up and childish in many ways. When she complained that the Japanese were "cheap teachers" in the States, one mother who was herself a professional violinist said, "As a high-school graduate, she should be studying, not teaching." Kako was masterful in playing on people's emotions, in working on their sympathies to gain her own ends. An interesting young woman and a good teacher of children, partly because she was childlike herself!

Chapter XIII

Miscellany

Children are mirrors—they reflect what comes to them. They are more influenced by what we *do* than by what we *say*, as shown by a child's answers to questions about the function of a traffic light:

> Red light—"Stop"
> Green light—"Go"
> Yellow light—"Go faster"

"Actions speak louder than words" applies to more than children. Imagine my surprise when several long-time critics of Suzuki and his violinists suddenly advertised a Suzuki Workshop for their school!

Once when I was speaking of the difference between music as part of oneself (memorized, absorbed) and music as part of a stand (outside, not mastered), a musician said "Taking the printed music away from a symphony player is like taking the bottle away from a baby!" A line from a Greek movie went: "Which birds learned to sing by reading?" Perhaps our aim should be to try to play violin the way birds fly and fish swim.

A bit weary of being asked "When do they learn to read?" my reply is that "Seitz-reading" comes in Volume 4 of the Suzuki Violin Method. I recall an experience with sight-reading in Koriyama, near Nara.

After a pleasant askanabe dinner in a doctor's home, it was suggested that we sight-read a bit. We started on a baroque work for two violins, with two players on each part. Suddenly one of the parts fell off the stand. I put down my violin and stooped to pick up the part, but I noticed that the two players "reading" from the fallen part went right on playing, without missing a note. I deliberately stayed down near the floor for several minutes, admiring the players' skill in "sight-reading" or complete grasp of style, or whatever it should be called! Our Japanese friends are not above pulling "a fast one," and they do it with a very straight face.

There seems to be a rather common philosophy today that if we just do enough things *badly*, they will add up to something *good*. The truth, however, can be expressed this way:

$$100 \times 0 = 0$$
$$1 \times 1 = 1$$

In a Japanese newspaper I read an article about the "ostentatious waste" of Occidentals, in the eyes of Orientals. This certainly applies to the common Western practice of learning a piece, playing it once, then dropping it forever. In Talent Education what is learned continues to be used and built upon, and is not discarded. The "Journey of *Perpetual Motion*" in Talent Education, for example, goes thus: Original form, then 2 bows, then add second part; through keys of A, D, G; then begin with first finger halfstep above open strings, go up by halfsteps through seventh position; use spiccato and other more advanced bowings. And so on!

Miss Numanami claimed that the Japanese speak "from the neck up," very staccato and fast. The way they talk is the way they play. The Japanese language is not good for singing or singers—the people and language are better suited to *instrumental* music than vocal.

Suzuko Hillyer, wife of violist Rafael Hillyer and a graduate of Toho School, thinks the Orientals have taken to the violin "because of the discipline needed for violin study. Oriental discipline suits the violin," newspapers report her as saying. "And Japanese children tend to have thin fingers, which helps them produce pure pitch. Besides, the Japanese are good at small details, like making small transistor radios. And small details is what violin practice is all about." I heartily agree with her analysis!

Charles K. Parker, who taught school in Japan for many years, wrote in *The Berkshire Eagle* (Pittsfield, Massachusetts):

> Suzuki's influence is due in large measure to the fact that in Oriental thought there is a positive—one might almost say dynamic—reverence for the teacher and master. (CC—Of Confucius, "The Master said—." Of Suzuki, "Sensei said—.") Suzuki has achieved the status of a great teacher and master and that is why he has thousands of disciples. He has established a way of life—a new way of life for the younger generation.
>
> Japanese psychology demands that one play a role and follow a way of life. This is what all Japanese understand by personality; hence the utter devotion of Suzuki's violin students and the extraordinary musical feeling which so many of his young disciples have shown.
>
> These Japanese children are not taking music lessons. They are living.

During the years when Japanese children have made American tours I have attended many of their concerts. The program usually opens with a group playing part of the Eccles "Sonata." The first two tones are enough to rivet the attention of the audience and set the mood of the entire program. This I saw again and again! The children don't miss a trick in these concerts. Some music teachers make disparaging remarks ("Trained seals," etc.), but I have never seen an audience that was not completely captivated by them.

Guru Maharishi Hahesh Yogi teaches "transcendental meditation"—a kind of relaxed focusing of the mind on its *clear, uncluttered center*—a discipline he advocates to cure the world's woes. "For world peace, we have to have peace for the individual." Mr. Suzuki often speaks of peace for the world, also, and of how it depends on improving *people*.

Zen

I have often thought of the connections between Zen Buddhism and Talent Education. (A leading writer on Zen is also named Suzuki, *Dr. D. T.*, from whom most of my information comes.) Daisetz Suzuki summed up all that he had written, experienced, or said: "The most important thing of all is love." Shinichi Suzuki titled the book of his life and teaching "Nurtured by Love." (The Oriental emphasis on peace and love is somewhat more convincing to American young people who do not remember Pearl Harbor than to some of the older generation who do.) James Reston rather cynically headed a recent column: "Love makes the world—overpopulated?"

A friend claims that plants and animals respond to love. His son hates goats, and treats them roughly. When he milks them they give much less milk than they do for his father, who loves them, talks to them, pats them. The same is true with plants, trees, etc.—they respond as they are treated. Isn't this true of *all* life, or living things?

Liberation of the mind from clutter is like the sculptor creating by taking away, by liberating the stone (or the violin-maker liberating the block of wood to attain the top or back of a violin). Simplicity, lack of complications—playing without notes, music-stand, or chair (yes, even without *shoes*—how firm a foundation!) gets closer to the fundamentals or basics in music.

The world is not going anywhere and there is *no hurry*. In art, hurry and all it involves, is fatal. People in a hurry cannot feel or think clearly.

The major problem in all disciplines is to bring the student to the point from which he can really begin. (Suzuki: "Now you're ready to start lessons on this piece.") The sumi-e brush must draw "by itself," with unhesitating spontaneity—with constant practice, but no effort. (Suzuki: "The bow-hair must play by itself—don't think so much!")

A sudden, instantaneous quality to the view of the world gives total presence of mind; there is no other time than *this instant*. The "eternal now" does not come from anywhere, is not going anywhere. (So it is with the training of concentration in Talent Education, and the refusal to be a "slave to the clock.")

West: Divide and conquer. East: Unify and live. Zen's pursuit of psychological wholeness aims to achieve a thoroughly integrated man without a divided mind. Egolessness, non-interference by the conscious mind, an immovable center with great motility all around it, immediateness of action, an uninterrupted movement of life-energy—these concepts were taught in fencing and applied to violin playing also.

Zen is a *depth* religion of the here and now, *this moment* —not a horizontal, expansionist religion emphasizing a future life and always new experiences. Many parallels can be drawn between Talent Education as contrasted with Western education and Zen Buddhism as contrasted with Christianity.

Zen gives importance to beauty and art in life, emphasizes quality rather than quantity, feeling more than technique. (What can be said about the religious sects which considered the violin to be an "instrument of the Devil," and forbade its use in church?)

Ear-learning (viva voce) is the traditional way music has been taught in the Orient. The sharp ears and quick reproduction of what is heard are common. Note the Indian musicians' eagerness and delight in immediately playing back the most complicated melodies and rhythms. Improvisation, as well as imitation, is featured. (Not only musical improvisation, but improvisation in programming, teaching, etc.) This adds freshness and charm, and avoids rigid over-rehearsing and stiff, formal programming and presentation. The Japanese don't just imitate. They take over what appeals to them and then *improve* it!

Early Start

The best place to start improving education is at the beginning, not the end. There is hope for better results starting with the very young child rather than with the graduate student. Much of the recent trouble caused by college students is a result of the miserable "education" they received when young.

Japanese Talent Education students are not the only Orientals who begin violin study very early. Two outstanding young Korean artists started early, Kyung Wha Chung at four and Young Uck Kim at five. Very young children always attract the most attention at public concerts. I remember one of our little three-year-olds in the front row who picked her nose on stage—a real show-stopper! We have had "pools of living water" on stage several times and, as concert time approaches, the parade of young violinists with their mothers to the rest rooms is something to see.

I observed a student teacher in an Elementary School working on reading with one of the slowest children in our Suzuki program. She had some problems teaching reading, but the boy's fundamentals—form, tone, and pitch—were ten times better than those of the children in the public-school class who had been taught reading *first*. The quality of his playing had been stressed more than the quantity of pieces played.

Games and Tests

These are used for specific purposes in Talent Education. They are also used in group sessions when the children are tiring. They are not the main feature of the teaching, as implied in a public school class I once saw walking around the room as their teacher explained to me, "Suzuki method!" (When Mr. Hirose was asked by some teachers what was the first thing he taught a child at the start of lessons, he replied "To bow." This was taken as a joke, but it *wasn't*. The mutual respect shown by pupil and teacher in the customary bow at the beginning and end of each lesson in Japan is something which would help American education.)

Now for a few examples. For *preparation* (to get the motor going, to come to life, to jack up reactions, or start on self-control): Teacher counts during "planting" of child, while child holds violin without left hand, or during development of long bow stroke. Children yell back at the teacher, "let go." *Fast* gymnastics, following teacher's lead—hand up to top of head; hands slap sides; jump *after*, then *with*, the teacher. *Race* in picking up the violin and bow from floor and starting to play. Play dictation back from teacher—"echo." Teacher says "I can't hear you," as he goes farther back in the hall or blocks a child's ears. With left hand in playing position, thumb and pinky make a "spy-glass"—child looks through it and sees first finger as it reaches back for a low tone.

For *secure hold of violin* without left hand: Teacher counts, as above. Children shake hands (left hands, of course) during open strings while playing Variations. Walk, stoop, play on left leg only while swinging right one. Hop on one leg.

For *control of bow* (tip, especially): Rocket blastoff,

windshield wiper, antenna (bow goes up on top of child's head), bow becomes extension of child's nose, ear, chin—following teacher's lead. Play in dark room—turn off lights or close eyes. Play holding bow at tip, or by hair (with Kleenex) near frog.

For *tempo* and *unison rhythm*: March in tempo. Clap on one, count other beats silently—or one, two, three (silent) four (clap).

For *mastery* (and jacking up reactions): Divide group into halves, "change sides" in playing, on teacher's clap (but not until clap actually *sounds*) while playing Vivaldi "Concerto" or other piece. (One half of whole group plays at a time.) One person fingers, another bows the same violin—add pairs, change partners, change from right to left-hand part—while playing Fiocco "Allegro" or other piece. Play Bach "Double Concerto," march as teacher switches players on parts, one by one. Answer questions, do math problems, count ceiling lights, or read aloud while playing, without faltering, a concerto or other piece. "Instant programming" —play any piece in repertoire at any time, as called for by teacher. Play any piece from its opening rhythm, as shown by teacher's clapping, bow motion in the air, or knocking on the back of the violin.

Criticisms

It has been my experience that many people seem to be looking for something to criticize about the Japanese people in general and Mr. Suzuki in particular, and most especially, his Talent Education. I'll now oblige such readers!

An example of the difference in ways of thinking between East and West: Former Ambassador to Japan Edwin Reischauer says that he and his wife had once invited some Japanese friends to their home in Tokyo for dinner. One

couple did not show up. Later, when the Reischauers in-
quired about their absence, the missing friends explained,
"We had a previous engagement. We didn't want to offend
you. If we had told you we couldn't come and then didn't
show up, we would have offended you *twice!*"

Newspapers recently carried the story of Japan's Ambassador to Argentina being fired because he wrote that the
Japanese are "childlike" and not much more attractive than
pygmies and Hottentots. He also wrote that the Japanese
have a proverbial lack of a sense of humor. He detected a
great resurgence of nationalism in the minds of the Japanese,
and said they were gaining confidence and self-reliance.
"I think the Japanese racial complex and sense of inferiority
to Westerners is very deep, almost incurable."

The Japan Times in April of 1955 carried an article
headed "Mass 'Talent Education' System Comes Under
Strong Fire" by Kyoko Matsumoto. Here are a few quotes:

> This new method, however, will do more harm than good to
> society as long as the general circumstances of this country are
> not prepared for it.
>   The Suzuki Method is, broadly speaking, a spiritual education
> —cultivation of sensibility—rather than a physical teaching of
> technique. Moral strength such as endurance and will power is as
> much an important factor.
>   M. Mashino of the Primary School Section of the Ministry
> of Education criticizes: It requires attendance of parents at
> children's lessons. Therefore, it is only children of privileged
> families who can afford to receive lessons and those children are
> liable to become victims of their parents who force children into
> severe training just to satisfy their own vanity. If Talent Educa-
> tion went too far in disregard of children's ability, music would
> no longer be a joy but a burden. It is charged that the system
> has unduly stirred the vanity of and a stiff rivalry among parents.
> They exert much pressure upon the children as possible future
> money earners such as were seen among juvenile jazz singers and
> movie stars. The fact that parents are more enthusiastic than
> some of the pupils may well prove the defect inherent in this

sort of educational system. Mashino added that there were not
so many countries in the world where the Talent Education
system was so enthusiastically advocated as in Japan.

Other forms of Talent Education are listed. The mushrooming
of more than 100 ballet schools in Tokyo after the war is evidence
of parents' zeal. 'Child-prodigy-painters' have been created with
the support of journalism. Private painting schools kill the crea-
tive power of children, through imitation in painting to win the
prize. At home parents tend to overspend their income for the
'art education' of their children and as a result lower the living
standard.

Wilma Salisbury wrote a review of a workshop concert,
"Tot Concert at Oberlin Is Unusual," for the Cleveland *Plain
Dealer* of June 30, 1968. Here is a short critical section from
this review:

Suzuki's method has been phenomenally successful in training
thousands of children to play the violin, but many music teachers
still regard it with suspicion. There is nothing artistic about playing by ear and copying someone else's style, they say. There is
something stifling about giving every child exactly the same
repertory in exactly the same sequence. One noted musician
(Isaac Stern) criticized the method because it had engendered
relatively few concert violinists.

Suzuki, however, is not primarily concerned with developing
professional musicians. His purpose is to give music to every
child and to develop the full potential of each student.

Donal Henahan closed his review of the New York
recital debut of Mr. Suzuki's student, Miss Yukari Tate
(*The New York Times*, November 5, 1968): "As yet, however, Miss Tate does not seem to have broken out of the
excellent-student category." Yukari Tate *did* play better
in Oberlin than in New York, I think, after hearing her in
both places. But what Mr. Henahan could not know, naturally, was that after leaving Oberlin, she had a bad fall in
Chicago and could not play at all for a while. Coming not

long before her New York date, this did not permit her to
be in top form for her New York recital.

Professor Steven Staryk in an article, "String Shortage,"
in the *Oberlin Alumni Magazine* for November, 1969, writes
this paragraph:

> The only partially successful group method of violin teaching
> thus far has been that of Shinichi Suzuki, and this is effective
> only up to a primitive level. The primary contribution of this
> system in fact has been the tapping of a new source of potential
> violin talent in Japan. Its success, also, is due largely to the social,
> economic and cultural environments of the Orient, an atmo-
> sphere not unlike that of Eastern Europe which produced the
> majority of the last generation of violinists, and still continues to
> produce the vast majority of those of the present. Whether by
> heritage or by necessity, East Europe, Japan and other Far East
> nations share a seriousness of character, determination and
> racial qualities sympathetic to the stringed instrument. A most
> interesting account of this comparison was published by *Time*
> newsmagazine, Nov. 3, 1967, page 46.

Professor Staryk's opening statement about a "group
method of violin teaching" shows that he is not acquainted
with the Suzuki Method. It's the same old story—many
people have seen pictures of large numbers of Japanese
children playing together, and assume that the children are
taught that way. They aren't—they are taught in careful,
individual lessons. (It is true that Professor Staryk and Mr.
Suzuki were on the panel of judges for the 1969 Montreal
International Music Competition. At that time Professor
Staryk showed Mr. Suzuki his valuable violin and bows,
and played a scale for him.)

Professor David Dawson of Indiana University gave me
his analysis: "Orientals work so darned hard!" (Not a bad
habit.)

When I hear the criticism that the young Japanese violinists don't really know what they are doing, or a statement
like this, "The main purpose of Talent Education is to sell

violins and books," I suspect that the wine being served comes from sour grapes!

The Educational Director of a publishing company said recently that there is some feeling that Talent Education in the States is becoming a "cult," and that the Board of Directors of Talent Education, U.S.A. is a closed corporation, out to make money for itself. This last statement made me wonder just how much of my own money I have spent in promoting Talent Education over the years.

Mr. Suzuki, his young artists, and his ideas are now exerting a profound impact on American education. California already requires the broadening of early childhood education to encompass children of pre-kindergarten age. Public school kindergartens will become mandatory in Florida's elementary schools in 1973, but early education won't stop there. Schools Superintendent Dr. Raymond Shelton of Hillsborough County, Florida, anticipates experimental classes with three- or four-year-olds in this decade, as a forerunner of what will become the standard beginning level for education "in this next generation." And individualized instruction will mean new and varied attempts to teach each student at his own level—not at the class average. Having observed my grandchildren learn to read "on their own" before starting first grade, I question the validity of the concept of kindergarten as merely a place for children to play!

I close this chapter by quoting from an article I wrote in 1963, after observing Talent Education in action in Japan: "I offer my sincere opinion that Mr. Suzuki's Talent Education program appears to me to be the most significant and promising development in string education today. Furthermore, I believe firmly that his method and ideas deserve investigation and study by teachers of *all* subjects!" *In 1970, this statement still stands.*

Chapter XIV

Chronology of Experience With Talent Education

December 10, 1955—First Oberlin College-Community String Festival. One hundred and seventy-seven players in R. Vaughan Williams' *Concerto Grosso* included Kenji Mochizuki, violin.

Early 1958—Kenji Mochizuki showed Tokyo film in Oberlin (film made in Tokyo of the 1955 National Concert of Talent Education; hundreds of Japanese children playing Bach "Double Concerto"). Mr. Suzuki and Dr. Honda sent books, programs, tapes, pictures. Miyako Matsuki, my violin student, helped translate books and studied them. In May, Kenji showed the Talent Education film at a meeting in Oberlin of the Ohio String Teachers Association. John Kendall and Robert Klotman were in the audience.

November-December, 1959—*Music Educators Journal* contained my article, "Japanese String Festival."

Spring, 1963—Visited Mr. Suzuki and Talent Education centers in Japan for six weeks.

July 4, 1963—*A Summary of My Impressions of Talent Education in Japan*, pamphlet printed in Tokyo and distributed at International Society for Music Education Conference held in Tokyo. (Also printed in the *Oberlin News-Tribune*, and contained essentially in my article, "Genius by the Gross," in *Oberlin Alumni Magazine*, May, 1964.)

September 27, 1963—Gave program on "Saino-Kyoiku in Japan" for Oberlin Woman's Club. Hiroko Yamada played Mozart-Kreisler "Rondo."

September 30, 1963—Discussion of Suzuki Violin Method at organizational meeting, Oberlin Conservatory. Following this, Miss Yamada and I started about thirty children on violin.

We gave many club programs on Talent Education and Japan.

March 1, 1964—Miss Yamada played the Saint-Saens "Introduction and Rondo Capriccioso" with the Elyria Little Symphony, which I was conducting at the time. Elyria, Ohio.

March 15, 1964—Co-Chairman, MENC-ASTA session presenting Suzuki and ten Japanese children, Sheraton Hotel, Philadelphia, Pa. Gave my Summary at end of program. What a pleasure this occasion was, after I had written in 1959: "Perhaps Mr. Suzuki and a number of Japanese youngsters might appear at one of our national meetings?"

March 16, 1964—Two Oberlin sessions with Mr. Suzuki, Dr. Honda, Kenji Mochizuki, and ten Japanese children, plus about twenty-six of ours on the "Variations" in the afternoon.

April 28, 1964—Talent Education program for the Oberlin City Club. Children played the "Variations."

May, 1964—Cover picture and my article, "Genius by the Gross," in *Oberlin Alumni Magazine*. My article, "Suzuki in Oberlin," in *Orchestra News*.

May 31, 1964—Final program of the year by Oberlin Young Violinists (23), Studio Theater. "Allegro" (Suzuki) most advanced piece. (Allegro-*joyful*. "Smile when you play that, pardner!") In developing a longer stroke of the bow on "Long, Long Ago" I sometimes say "Now play *Long, Long A-Bow*." Children laugh; such gags appeal to them and help in getting an idea across.

June 29, 1964—Led a Graduate Seminar on Strings at the

New England Conservatory, Boston, Mass. About thirty teachers attended.

October 30, 1964—Our Suzuki Class gave a program for a teachers' convention at the Toledo (Ohio) Museum of Art. Fifteen children played; "Allegro" most advanced. Miss Yamada and Miss Toba now teaching. Miss Yamada played Chausson "Poème" while Monet slides were shown, in a session planned by Boris Nelson.

November 18, 1964—Suzuki program for a teachers' meeting, Bucyrus, Ohio. Six children played, "Etude" (Suzuki) most advanced piece.

January 16, 1965—Sixth Oberlin College-Community String Festival. String orchestra of 135, including the two Japanese teachers, played the Bloch "Concerto Grosso" with Norman Lloyd, piano. Thirty Suzuki children played a group of pieces; "Allegretto" (Suzuki) most advanced.

February 27, 1965—Yamada and Toba gave Suzuki Workshop at Oberlin for teachers of District 4 of OMEA.

March 12, 1965—I gave program on "Japanese Talent Education" for Michigan String Teachers Association, Oakland University, Michigan.

April 11, 1965—*Fine Arts* magazine contained my article, "Oberlin College Imports the Suzuki Method."

April–May, 1965, *Music Educators Journal* contained my article, "Suzuki in Oberlin."

May 1, 1965—Program of solos by children.

June 6, 1965—Final Suzuki program for semester. Thirty-two children played; "Hunters' Chorus" (Weber) most advanced piece. Last appearance for Yamada and Toba. One disappointment I often had in our program came from children moving away—sometimes to a place where no teacher was available or where instruction was inferior. It is sad to see children go "down hill," especially when they have a good start and show promise.

June 14–17, 1965—Served as advisor on film about Suzuki made by the University of Illinois at Monticello College, Godfrey, Illinois.

June 25–July 17, 1965—Directed Suzuki Workshop for String Teachers in new Oberlin Conservatory building. Mr. and Mrs. Suzuki and Yuko Honda here. 120 teachers from twenty-five states and four provinces of Canada attended. Twenty-five students had lessons. Public program given July 14:

Suzuki Workshop Program

"Japanese Carpenter's Song and Nagoya Lullaby"
    Shinichi Suzuki, violin

"La Folia" .... Corelli-Suzuki
    Yuko Honda, violin
    Carolyn Bridger, piano

Tone Studies by Workshop Participants
    Jenny Cramer, violin
    Camille Cashatt, viola
    Sister Ellen Marie, violin
    Candy Wheeler, violin

"Duo for Violin and Viola" (K. 423) .... Mozart
    Allegro
    Adagio
    Rondo-Allegro
        Mrs. Dorothy Mauney, violin
        John Cox, viola

Chorus from *Judas Maccabeus* .... Handel
    Sanae and Yukie Ieda, violins

Menuetto No. 2 .... Bach

Allegretto   ⎫
Perpetual Motion ⎬ .... SUZUKI
Allegro   ⎭

"Long, Long Ago" .... BAYLY

"Lied" .... German Folk Song
    Young Violinists from Oberlin, Put-In-Bay, and
    Cleveland Classes. Mrs. Patricia Cooley, piano.

"Variations on Twinkle, Twinkle, Little Star" .. SUZUKI
    Young Violinists and Teachers
        Mr. Suzuki, piano

August–September, 1965—*The School Musician* contained
    my article, "National Concert in Japan."
Fall, 1965—Eiko Suzuki arrived from Japan.
December, 1965, *Oberlin Alumni Magazine* contained my
    article, "Suzuki Workshop."
December 4, 1965—Suzuki Class Program in Kulas Recital
    Hall. *"Hunters' Chorus"* most advanced piece.
January 29, 1966—My class solo recital. Twelve played. Vi-
    valdi A Minor Concerto (I) most advanced piece.
February, 1966—Gave Suzuki Clinic for Texas String Teach-
    ers Association, Dallas, Texas.
April 28, 1966—Suzuki Program for Station WVIZ-TV, Cleve-
    land, Ohio. Music included Menuettos by Beethoven
    and Boccherini, played by Paul Chou and Elaine Pea-
    cock, respectively, and Bach's "Loure," played by Eiko
    Suzuki. Videotape shown many times to Cleveland area
    school children.
May 9, 1966—Gave two Suzuki Concerts in Huntington area,
    Long Island, New York. Same performers as for above
    TV program.
May 29, 1966—End of year concert, Warner Hall. More

than seventy children played. Of seven solos, the Vivaldi A Minor Concerto (I) with string quartet accompaniment was most advanced. Of ten group selections, "The Two Grenadiers" by Schumann was most advanced. Eiko Suzuki played the Bloch "Nigun."

July 20-23, 1966—Guests of Eastman School at their Suzuki Institute for String Teachers. Eiko Suzuki played Tchaikovsky "Concerto" three times.

Fall, 1966—Kazuko Numanami arrived from Japan.

October, 1966. Tour Program of Japanese children contained short article I had written. I heard the children in Philharmonic Hall, New York City, October 9.

October 21, 1966—Eiko Suzuki played Saint-Saens "Introduction and Rondo Capriccioso" with Orchestra which I conducted in Mansfield, Ohio, at a teachers' convention.

December 10, 1966—Seventh Oberlin College-Community String Festival. String orchestra of 120, including Eiko and Kazuko, played R. Vaughan Williams "Concerto Grosso." About seventy Suzuki children played thirteen pieces; Handel "Bourrée" was most advanced.

December 11, 1966—Suzuki program for Cleveland Oberlin Woman's Club, Plymouth Church, Shaker Heights, Ohio. Fourteen children with Alumni connections performed. Seitz "Rondo" from 5th Concerto most advanced.

January 6-7, 1967—Two Suzuki programs for Ohio Music Educators Association Convention, Sheraton-Columbus Hotel, Columbus, Ohio. Twenty-seven children played first program, thirty-two second. Handel "Bourrée" most advanced group number; Bach "Double Concerto" (I) and Weber *"Country Dance"* most advanced solos. Kazuko and Eiko played Mendelssohn and Sibelius Concerti.

April 19, 1967—Participated in *Symposium on Early Child-*

hood Musical Education, session on "The Suzuki Approach in America Today." Playhouse of The Henry Street Settlement, New York City.

April 28, 1967—Gave two Clinics on "Adapted Suzuki Materials for String Class Instruction" and "The Use of Suzuki Materials for String Class Instruction," using local high-school players and Paul Chou, Allentown, Pennsylvania.

June 19—July 1, 1967—Director of Suzuki Workshop for String Teachers, Oberlin Conservatory, with Mr. Suzuki, Eiko Suzuki, and Kazuko Numanami. About seventy teachers from twenty-one states and two Canadian provinces, fifty-three children for lessons. Concert June 23, "Two Grenadiers" most advanced group number, Bach A Minor Concerto (I) most advanced solo.

July 24—August 4, 1967—Led Suzuki Workshop at Idaho State University, Pocatello, Idaho.

September 23–24, 1967—Attended Directors' meeting of Talent Education, U.S.A., at Northern Illinois University, DeKalb, Illinois.

October 24, 1967—Introduced touring Suzuki children from Japan in concert at Bedford High School, Bedford, Ohio.

December 3, 1967—Gave Suzuki program for Oberlin Alumni Club of Detroit, Mercy College, Detroit, Michigan. Eiko and Kazuko played; I spoke on "Saino-Kyoiku."

January 28, 1968—About thirty-five of our Suzuki children played for Oberlin Alumni from Summit and Portage counties, Congregational Church of Silver Lake (Akron), Ohio. Twelve group pieces, "Humoresque" most advanced.

February 23, 1968—Eiko Suzuki played Brahms "Concerto" with Oberlin Orchestra, after winning competition.

May 11, 1968—Warner Hall Concert by about fifty-five

children, dedicated to Eiko. Fifteen group pieces, Bach "Double Concerto" with Mauney String Quartet most advanced.

May 27, 1968—Eiko's farewell recital in Kulas Hall: Mozart "Sonata in E minor," Chausson "Poème," Bartok "Rumanian Dances," Tartini " 'Devil's Trill' Sonata."

June 24–29, 1968—Director, Suzuki Method Workshop for Teachers, Oberlin Conservatory, with Kazuko Numanami. Forty-one teachers from fourteen states, about fifty children from five states. Public concert June 28, Bach "Loure" and Vivaldi A minor Concerto (I) with organ and string ensemble most advanced group numbers. All music in ten volumes of Suzuki Violin Method performed live or on tape at Workshop, and all volumes taped by Kazuko (1-4) and Eiko (5-10). Cleveland *Plain Dealer* review of concert by Wilma Salisbury June 30.

July 1–5, 1968—Taught Suzuki ideas in graduate course, "Contemporary Concepts of String Teaching," at Northwestern University School of Music, Evanston, Illinois.

July 31, 1968—Led Suzuki Workshop for Robert Flanik's students and their parents, Lyndhurst, East Cleveland, Ohio.

September 20–21, 1968—Gave four Suzuki programs with Elaine Peacock for Council of Arts and Sciences for Central Florida, Orlando, Florida.

October 20–21, 1968—Tenth Anniversary Celebration of Talent Education in the United States, at Oberlin. Workshop with our children. Concert by touring Japanese children. Kenji Mochizuki showed his original film, first shown here ten years ago. Clinic session with Seiichi Sanpei and Hitomi Kasuya. Yukari Tate, Mrs. Yuko Hirose in United States Debut Recital: Vitali "Chaconne," Grieg Sonata in C Minor, Chausson "Poème,"

Paganini Concerto No. 1 in D Major, Suk "Four Pieces."
Meeting of Board of Talent Education, U.S.A. Reviews
of children's concert by Theodore Price in the *Akron-
Beacon-Journal* (October 21) and by Boris Nelson in
the *Toledo Blade* (October 27). 1968 tour program contained my "A Memorable 10th Anniversary." (A picture
of the children taken at this celebration was used on the
cover of the 1969 tour program. Arthur E. "Pinky" Prince-
horn, photographer for Oberlin College from 1930–1969,
took several hundred fine photographs of our Suzuki activities through the years.)

December 6, 1968—"Home-Made Suzuki" program for Oberlin Woman's Club, First Church. Twelve children from
seven families, twenty performers altogether. First appearance for two young cellists in our program. Vivaldi
G minor Concerto (I) most advanced solo piece; Haydn
"Gipsy Rondo" for piano trio most advanced ensemble
number.

January 17, 1969—Gave program with Molly Fung (four
years old) and her mother, Rotary Club, Oberlin Inn.

January 8–29, 1969—Led a Winter Term Project on Suzuki
Method, fifteen hours of instruction.

April 5, 1969, *String Along* (Bulletin of Ohio String Teachers Association) contained my article, "Home-Made Suzuki."

April 20, 1969—Gave Suzuki program for Ohio String Teachers Association at Kent State University, Kent, Ohio.
Fifty children played. Seitz "Allegretto moderato" from
2nd Concerto most advanced group number. Vivaldi G
minor Concerto (Finale) and Weber "Country Dance"
most advanced solos.

May 18, 1969—Final concert of year in Warner Hall. At
least fifty-five children played (out of eighty studying).

Seitz "Allegretto moderato" played by group and solos included Fiocco "Allegro" and Vivaldi G minor Concerto Finale.

In the procession of performances by Oberlin children, it may be noted how very gradual is the progression to new pieces. Growth appears not only in the addition of new pieces, but also in the constantly better sound and performance of the old ones. Improvement comes by doing *better* what we have done before, as well as by doing *new* things.

The Japanese teachers who are themselves graduates of Talent Education go *very* slowly and carefully. They say the most common fault in the American application of the method is going *too fast*. We often hear of a child playing a Vivaldi Concerto after only one year of study —but *how* is the Vivaldi or anything else played? Usually, *atrociously!*

May 24, 1969—Solo program, through Dittersdorf *German Dance.*

Spring, 1969—Book, "Nurtured by Love," by Shinichi Suzuki is published by Exposition Press, Jericho, New York. Translation by Waltraud Suzuki. The most complete exposition available of his ideas and life, written by Mr. Suzuki himself. Oberlin mentioned several times.

July 16–18, 1969—Presented three Suzuki sessions at American String Teachers Association-Indiana University Conference, Indiana University, Bloomington, Indiana. Worked with children from St. Charles School in Bloomington and from the University of Louisville, Kentucky. Four Oberlin children and two mothers played. Cindy Mauney and Elaine Peacock each played a complete Vivaldi "Concerto"; together they played the Bach "Double Concerto." Some sixty or seventy teachers present.

July–August, 1969—Two-week trip to Japan for Summer School in Matsumoto and time in Tokyo. (Written up in Chapter X.)

September 27, 1969—Led Workshop for Ishpeming-Negaunee Community School, Negaunee, Michigan. More than eighty students, from Senior High School Orchestra to small beginning Suzuki children.

October 13, 1969—Attended Workshop and Concert by touring Japanese children in Marion, Ohio.

After hearing many American children in various Suzuki programs over the years, I note that a common weakness is this: The ending of the final tone of a piece (and often of phrases within the piece) is careless and needs attention! *No piece is ended until its last tone is finished, not just started.* In group playing, many final tones are not ended together, but "yanked off" at different times and in different ways by the young players.

October 26, 1969—Meeting of Talent Education Board in Chicago, Illinois.

Fall-Winter, 1969–70—Writing this book, in Oberlin and Florida, home of the mockingbird, "The Prima Donna of Talent Education."

February 17, 1970—Spoke to Music Teachers of Tampa Area Public Schools on "Suzuki Talent Education," Tampa, Florida.

March 6, 1970—Gave lecture on "The Suzuki Approach to Violin Playing" at University of South Florida, Tampa, Florida.

Spring, 1970—*Talent Education, A Program for Early Development* by Masaaki Honda, published by EDA 1-4-3 Magome Ohta-ku Tokyo (143) Japan. Dr. Honda's booklet is a valuable contribution, dealing with the history, definition and other items concerning Talent Education.

July 13–17, 1970—Conducted Graduate String Workshop at

Peabody Conservatory of Music, Baltimore, Maryland.

Finale

On May 1, 1968, I had sent the following letter of recommendation to an Oberlin College faculty committee:

Dear President Carr:

I should like to suggest Shinichi Suzuki for an honorary degree at Oberlin's 1969 Commencement. Now 70, Mr. Suzuki has led a rich and fruitful life, always closely associated with the violin.

Member of a prominent family of musicians and violin makers, he was born in Nagoya, Japan, where he worked in his father's violin factory and studied with Japanese violin teachers. After further study in other Japanese music centers, he went with Prince Tokugawa to Berlin, where he studied for a number of years with Karl Klingler and other German musicians. In Berlin he met his wife, Waltraud, a German singer.

On returning to Japan, Mr. Suzuki formed with three of his brothers a string quartet which toured extensively in Japan and introduced Western chamber music to many audiences. He taught violin in universities in Tokyo, Yokohama, and elsewhere—to students of college age by traditional methods.

His first experiment in teaching violin to a young child was with Toshiya Eto, then four years old. Eto is now an international concert artist, teacher at Curtis Institute, and musical man of the world.

It was not until the end of World War II that he decided to devote his life to the musical education of young children. Recovering from a serious illness, he observed how his sister's babies learned to speak Japanese. Applying this "mother tongue" method to teaching the violin to the little children whose war suffering stirred his compassion, Mr. Suzuki began his work with six young children and one violin.

As the results of his work became evident, more parents and teachers became interested, his manuals and recordings appeared and violins of all sizes became available. Talent Education became strongly established in Japan.

Through the years thousands of young Japanese children have learned to play the violin well under the teaching of Suzuki and the many teachers he has trained, now located in centers throughout Japan. Many brilliant performers have been produced, although the primary purpose of Talent Education is not to train professionals but to enrich the lives of children.

Today Mr. Suzuki's work is known the world over. He has done more than any other living person to stimulate a popular renewal of interest and genuine accomplishment in the languishing field of violin study.

The now widespread American interest in his work began at Oberlin ten years ago. His three visits to Oberlin, on his first American tour with young Japanese children, and later for two summer workshops, have made him well-known here. He has also made a considerable contribution to Oberlin College in the young graduates of his Talent Education he has sent here to teach our children during the past five years.

I should consider it a privilege to present Shinichi Suzuki for an honorary degree from Oberlin College.

Sincerely,
Clifford Cook

This nomination was turned down without comment.

*   *   *

For my investment of time, money, and health in Talent Education through these years—yes, even for the many headaches and heartaches involved—I have no regrets. I believe I have made a greater contribution to the cause of the strings than I would have if I had devoted these years to practice on my own violin, pleasant though that would have been. I trust the future will prove me to have been right in this judgment.

*   *   *